SUPERSTARS

FOOTBALL'S ALL-TIME GREATS

by Wayne R. Coffey

Watermill Press

For my mother, Marion R. Coffey,
who always gives me love and always makes me proud

ACKNOWLEDGMENTS

The author gratefully acknowledges the following people for their valuable assistance in providing information for this book: Fran Connors, public relations assistant, National Football League; Nate Wallack, director of public relations, Cleveland Browns; Patrick McCaskey, assistant public relations director, Chicago Bears; Kathie Delaney, media services assistant, New York Giants; Marge Blatt, assistant public relations director, Baltimore Colts; Jack Geyer and Jerry Wilcox, directors of public relations, Los Angeles Rams; and Paula Vogel of Wide World Photos, for her help with the photo research.

And finally, heartfelt thanks to Frank Downs Coffey for his special help in times of need.

Table of Contents

JIM THORPE

The year was 1950. The question was: Who is the greatest football player of the 20th century?

To find out, the Associated Press took a poll of sports reporters throughout the country. One man stood alone. His name was Jim Thorpe.

Not long after, the A.P. put another question to its nationwide panel: Who is the greatest athlete of the 20th century? The answer was the same—Jim Thorpe. Nobody else was even close. The second-place finisher, a well-known baseball player by the name of Babe Ruth, had 86 votes. Jim Thorpe had 252.

Jim Thorpe—or Bright Path, as his people called him—was an American Indian. He was born in 1888. Even as a young boy on the Sac and Fox reservation in Oklahoma, Jim excelled in the rugged outdoor life. The elder tribesmen marveled at the way young Jim could run, jump, hunt, swim, wrestle, climb trees, and tame wild horses. "Bright Path will be like his great-grandfather, Black Hawk," the tribe predicted.

Black Hawk was a legendary warrior and chieftain of the Sac and Fox Indians. He was said to be a man whose physical skills were surpassed only by his courage. Jim never knew Black Hawk, but he glowed with pride when he heard stories about his great-grandfather. The youngster was honored to be compared with his fabled ancestor.

"I am no more proud of my career as an athlete," said Jim toward the end of his life, "than I am of the fact that I am a direct descendant of that noble warrior."

And that means a great deal, coming from the man who was voted the greatest athlete of the 20th century.

Jim's rise to athletic stardom began at Carlisle, a small Indian school in Pennsylvania. He first heard of Carlisle from a school representative who happened to be passing through Oklahoma. An adventurous sort, Jim was excited by the idea of attending school in a new and far-off territory. At the age of 16, he made the long journey east to Pennsylvania. That was in 1904. By the time he left in 1912, Jim had helped to make little Carlisle one of the greatest football schools in the country.

Jim had played a little football as a youngster, but it wasn't until he got to Carlisle that he really fell in love with the game. Not that anybody really noticed him. Standing only five feet tall and not weighing much more than 100 pounds, Jim didn't look much like a football player. Still, he loved the speed, strength, and agility the game required and watched the Carlisle varsity endlessly, dreaming of the day when he would get his chance to play.

He didn't have to wait very long. While playing on the reserve team for a couple of years, Jim's wiry, boyish body bloomed into a powerful, thickly muscled frame of six feet and 180 pounds. The Carlisle coach, Glenn "Pop" Warner, began to take notice.

Jim made the varsity in 1907. But with his limited experience, he still didn't know the game that well. Coach Warner taught him some of the finer points in practice, but didn't play him much in the games. The idleness drove Jim crazy. He desperately wanted to play. He finally got his chance in a late-season game against the University of Pennsylvania, when Carlisle's star halfback, Albert Payne, was injured.

"Get in there, Thorpe," bellowed Warner. "Here's your chance."

Jim made the most of it. On his second play from scrimmage, he bulled through the line, bolted through the secondary, and sprinted 75 yards for a touchdown. It was a most impressive debut for one of the greatest football stars of all time. And he wasn't finished yet. He ran over and around the frustrated Penn defense for two more touchdowns that day to lead Carlisle to a 26–6 rout.

Thorpe began to make a name for himself in 1908. While earning third-team All-America honors, he established himself as the most versatile performer anyone had ever seen on the gridiron. As a ball carrier, he had the devastating combination of blinding speed and awesome power. But that wasn't all. As a blocker, tackler, and kicker, Thorpe had few—if any—equals.

In addition, Jim excelled at every sport he tried. When he wasn't carrying the pigskin, he was a standout performer on the Carlisle track team. In track and field, too, his versatility was astonishing. Winning five events in a single meet was routine for him. His records included: high jump—6 feet, 5 inches; broad jump—23 feet, 6 inches; shot put—47 feet, 9 inches; javelin—138 feet; pole vault—10 feet, 8 inches; 100-yard dash—10 seconds; 120-yard high hurdles—15 seconds; and 440-yard run—51 seconds.

Jim also was a fine baseball player. In fact, he played two seasons in the semipro East Carolina League. In one season as a pitcher, Jim won 23 games in 25 outings. His ballplaying also earned Jim a little bit of money—$15 a week. Later, those dollars would haunt Jim Thorpe for the rest of his life.

In 1911, Jim was to have his greatest football season at Carlisle. Having grown by this time to 6-foot-1 and 190 pounds, Jim dominated every game he played and became the most talked-about football player in the nation.

In Carlisle's opening game that year, he ran for three touchdowns and kicked two extra points—in only 17 minutes of playing time! After that, Coach Warner mercifully decided to rest his great halfback. That performance set the tone for the entire season.

Thorpe charged for three more touchdowns in the next game against St. Mary's. The stage was set for the next game, against powerful Pittsburgh. Little Carlisle had been destroying the small schools it played. But many experts believed the Indians could not compete with the best teams in the country. And Pitt was one of the best.

Thorpe and his Carlisle teammates proved the experts wrong. Streaking for touchdowns of 53 and 45 yards, Thorpe led the way for a 17–0 triumph. It didn't seem to bother Thorpe that the Pittsburgh defense was keying on him all afternoon. Even with three and four players, Pitt couldn't contain him. Jim's stunning performance prompted one sportswriter to marvel, "Thorpe is everything they say he is . . . and more."

His fame grew with each game. Nobody had ever seen a runner with such speed and power. He became the most-feared player of his day—and rightly so. Thorpe could score from everywhere and break a game open single-handedly.

Jim Thorpe saved his greatest heroics of the 1911 season for the most important game of the year, against Harvard. The top-ranked team in college football in

4

Jim Thorpe: The pride of Carlisle and, many believe, the greatest athlete America has ever produced.

those days, the Crimson had won eight straight games against the finest squads in the country when Jim Thorpe and Carlisle came to Cambridge. The 25,000 fans who packed into the stadium saw Thorpe put on an awesome one-man show.

Playing with heavily taped legs—the result of plowing through defenses for a whole season—Thorpe went to work after Harvard scored to take a 6-0 lead. After running deep into Harvard territory, he kicked a 23-yard field goal, narrowing the score to 6-3.

Still in the first quarter, Thorpe lined up again for a field goal, this time from 43 yards out. The long boot sailed right through the goal posts, tying the score at six. Things went from bad to worse for heavily favored Harvard, which didn't expect the little Indian school to be such a difficult opponent. Late in the first half, Thorpe connected on yet another field goal from 37 yards. Carlisle took a 9-6 lead into half time. With his injured legs, Jim didn't do much running in the first half. But he more than made up for it with his phenomenal field-goal kicking.

Not about to concede anything, Harvard came out smoking in the second half. The Crimson team embarked on a long touchdown drive to regain the lead, 12-9. It was time for Thorpe to take charge. "Give me the ball. I'm going to run," he told the Carlisle quarterback.

And how he ran! Carry after carry, Thorpe pounded into the line and sprinted around the end. Shedding powerful Harvard tacklers like flies, he galloped a total of 70 yards for a touchdown. Carlisle led, 15-12.

Following a Harvard field goal, which tied the score once more, Carlisle mounted a push late in the game. But the drive stalled, and with the clock winding down, it appeared that the brilliantly played match would end in a tie.

Carlisle had only one last chance to pull out the victory. Jim Thorpe lined up for a 50-yard field goal attempt. "Nobody can hit a field goal from there," said one skeptical fan. "Not even Jim Thorpe."

The ball was placed down. Harvard charged in, desperately trying to block the kick. As players swarmed around him, Thorpe stepped into the ball with all his remaining strength. The ball rocketed into the air . . . and didn't come down until it had vaulted through the uprights. It was good! The fans were stunned. The entire Carlisle team ran onto the field to mob their hero.

Carlisle won, 18–15. Jim Thorpe had scored every point.

A little later, Thorpe was named the first-team, All-American halfback. Sports fans from coast to coast praised the peerless Indian athlete from Carlisle. It wasn't long before the whole world joined in.

The year was 1912. The place was Stockholm, Sweden. The occasion was the Olympic Games, the meeting of the greatest athletes from all corners of the globe. When it was all over, one man stood out as the greatest—Jim Thorpe.

In those games, Thorpe staged perhaps the greatest athletic performance of all time. He won both the pentathlon and the decathlon, the two most grueling competitions imaginable. In sweeping the five-event pentathlon and the ten-event decathlon, Thorpe far outdistanced every other athlete in the field.

"Sir," proclaimed Sweden's King Gustav, "you are the most wonderful athlete in the world."

"Jim Thorpe," said William Howard Taft, President of the United States, "is the highest type of citizen."

After his triumphant return to the states, which was celebrated with festive parades in numerous cities, Jim returned to Carlisle for his final year of college football. Not surprisingly, it was his greatest year ever.

The legend of Jim Thorpe was spreading as fast as he could run. In a game against Dickinson, Thorpe made what is probably the longest run in football history. Prepared to punt from behind his own goal posts (there were no well-defined end zones then), Thorpe got a bad snap from center. The ball sailed over his head. He quickly retrieved it, some 20 yards behind his own goal. And he started out. He dodged one tackler, then another, then bulled through a couple more. A brilliant cutback, a change of pace, and Thorpe was in the clear. Running over and around virtually every player on the Dickinson team, Thorpe had raced 120 yards for a touchdown!

Thorpe's performance that season was outstanding. His long, breathtaking dashes with the football continually dazzled his opponents, while leading Carlisle to one romp after another. Before a game against Pittsburgh, Pitt Coach Joe Thompson vowed, "We've got Thorpe figured out. He'll never run through us again."

The man named Bright Path made Thompson eat those words. Thorpe ran for two touchdowns, kicked a field goal and six extra points, and left a wake of fallen Pitt defenders behind him. There was, in fact, nothing to "figure out" about Thorpe. He was simply the fastest and strongest runner anyone had ever seen.

Thorpe capped his season with a routinely brilliant performance against the powerful Army team. After running for one touchdown and throwing an option pass for another, Thorpe shocked his opponents by faking a punt and running 90 yards for still another score. He concluded his day's work with a feat never before seen: Taking a kickoff, Thorpe bolted through the entire Army team for a 90-yard touchdown. But suddenly, the referee blew his whistle, calling an offside penalty on Carlisle. So Army kicked again. And what did Thorpe do? He returned it 95 yards for a touchdown.

"That's the longest run I've ever made for one touchdown," joked Jim to his teammates. "One hundred eighty-five yards!"

By season's end, the All-American had shattered every college scoring record. In the 1912 season alone, he scored 25 touchdowns and 198 total points!

Thorpe was on top of the world. But not for long. Suddenly, tragically, the self-made throne of the world's greatest athlete came tumbling down. It was discovered that Thorpe had played semipro baseball in 1909 and 1910. The Amateur Athletic Union (AAU) investigated the charges, knowing that if they were true, Thorpe would have to be stripped of his precious Olympic medals. For all Olympic athletes must be amateurs, and, technically, the small salary Thorpe had received for his baseball playing made him a professional.

Jim did not deny the charges. He did not know he had done anything improper. "I was not very wise to the ways of the world," Thorpe told the AAU. "I did not realize what I did was wrong. I hope I will be partly excused by the fact that I was simply an Indian schoolboy and did not know that what I was doing was wrong."

But Jim Thorpe wasn't excused. His medals were taken from him and given to the second-place finishers in the pentathlon and decathlon. But these men did not accept the hand-me-down honors. "These medals belong to Jim Thorpe," they said.

To this day, Jim's Olympic awards are kept in a permanently displayed case in Lausanne, Switzerland. His name was erased from the Olympic record books.

Many people were outraged by the actions of the AAU and Olympic Committee. But even public uproar from all over the world could not change the fateful decision.

Thorpe felt wronged, but he wasn't about to let that end his great athletic career. He went on to play professional baseball with the New York Giants, and also coached and starred for the Canton Bulldogs, a professional football team. Although pro football was disorganized back then, Thorpe didn't need a formal league to continue his unequaled exploits on the gridiron.

In 1920, a group of men got together to form the American Professional Football Association, the forerunner of the NFL. Jim Thorpe was named president. The league went through a lot of growing pains. Franchises came and went, and players shuffled from team to team.

Thorpe himself continued to be a standout performer for several different teams. The greatest player the game had ever known played right through until 1929, when he retired at the ripe old age of 41. He was later named to the Pro Football Hall of Fame.

Unfortunately, there are no detailed pro football records dating back that far, so there is no precise way to compare Thorpe to latter-day players. The only way we can judge his greatness is on the basis of what was written and said about him. Perhaps that's enough. Because it's almost universally agreed by those who saw him on the football field—running, kicking, blocking, and tackling

Jim frolics with his sons shortly after his retirement from football.

—that Jim Thorpe was the greatest player they had ever seen.

We don't know for sure whether Thorpe was as powerful as Jimmy Brown or as fast as O. J. Simpson. But we do know that, in his own era, he was in a class by himself. No doubt he would be in the same class, if he were playing today.

"Jim Thorpe," a long-time observer of his once said, "is unquestionably the greatest athlete of all time."

FRANK GIFFORD

There was nothing Frank Gifford couldn't do on the football field. His reputation as one of the best and most versatile players in football history is undisputed.

A recent inductee to the Pro Football Hall of Fame, Gifford was a first-round draft choice by the New York Giants in 1952. He came to the pros with a fine record, achieved during his brilliant All-American career at the University of Southern California.

In his senior year alone, Frank rushed for 841 yards, completed 32 of 61 passes, scored 7 touchdowns, and kicked 26 extra points and 2 field goals. He also was a standout defensive back, making him a two-way iron man who often played almost the entire 60 minutes.

The 6-foot-1, 195-pound rookie made an immediate impression on the Giants. "Gifford is one of the most versatile athletes I have ever seen," raved Coach Steve Owen. "He has hard running ability. He is an accurate passer, a strong blocker, a sensational receiver, a superior defensive back, and, with practice, he could become a consistent place-kicker." (It's a good thing Frank didn't excel at anything else—the coach was running out of superlatives!)

The Giants wasted no time putting their multi-talented rookie to good use. After a solid first year as a running back and kick-return man, Frank was a very busy—and very effective—two-way man in 1953.

Doubling as a running back and defensive back, he often played more than 50 minutes a game. There were other two-way players in the NFL then, but few of them approached Gifford's grueling, nonstop time on the field.

In addition to rushing for 157 yards and catching passes for 262 more, Gifford established himself as one of the finest defensive backs in the NFL. Week after week, he shackled many of the league's best receivers. His top status as a defensive back was confirmed when he was named to the Pro Bowl.

If Frank had continued the exhausting, 50-minute pace he maintained in 1953, his career simply could not have lasted very long. Fortunately, the old two-way platoon era was on the way out. Players became either offensive or defensive specialists. This confronted the Giant coaches with a pleasant problem—what to do with Frank Gifford. Should the versatile star be used to dodge tackles and catch passes, or to make tackles and intercept passes?

The decision was made by a strong-willed assistant coach, who joined the Giants in 1954 from West Point. The new assistant, who was in charge of the offense, promptly claimed Frank for *his* unit. There wasn't much of an argument—especially after everyone saw what Frank could do as a full-time offensive player. That coach, who changed the course of Frank's career, was a football mastermind by the name of Vince Lombardi. Lombardi remained with the Giants until 1959, when he left to lead the then-lowly Green Bay Packers to the greatest dynasty in NFL history.

"To me," said Frank, "Vince was the difference between my becoming a good pro player and just another halfback. He turned my life around. Anything I

14

The New York Giants' Mr. Versatility.

accomplished in this game, I owe to him. He was a very special man."

Under the direction of the late Lombardi, who is often credited with revolutionizing the running game in pro football, Gifford blossomed into one of the league's premier runners. In 1954, he picked up 368 yards on just 66 carries, good for a superb average of 5.6 yards per carry, and he also snared 14 passes for 154 yards. He was again named to the Pro Bowl, this time as a running back. Frank is the only man in NFL history to be named to the Pro Bowl as a defensive and offensive player in successive years.

After another fine season in 1955, when he was again chosen for the Pro Bowl, Gifford was sensational in 1956. Third in the league in pass receiving (51 catches) and fifth in the league in rushing (819 yards), Gifford was a unanimous choice as the NFL's Most Valuable Player. It was no coincidence that the Giants became one of the most dominant teams in the NFL. Sparked by Gifford's all-around brilliance, they captured the Eastern Conference title. Then, in the NFL championship game, the Giants walloped the Chicago Bears, 47–7. In addition to grabbing a 14-yard touchdown pass from quarterback Charley Conerly, Frank made several other dazzling catches, including a 67-yarder that helped put the Bears away for good. Frank rates it not only as his most memorable game, but as the game that helped catapult football to national prominence.

"Many people today allude to the 1958 title game, when we lost to Baltimore (23–17) in overtime, as the game that first brought pro football into the limelight," Frank noted. "I don't agree.

"I frankly think it was the 1956 game in New York. It wasn't even a sellout—there were only 56,000 people there. The next season the Giant's average attendance was *more* than 57,000 a game.

"It was in 1956," he explained, "when New York people and writers, who were baseball-oriented, began to realize football did exist. The advertising agencies began getting involved in it. The media was centered in New York, and everyone there began saying, 'Hey, football's here.'"

Whenever the turning point for football was, there is no question that Frank played an important part in it. Aside from his obvious talents on the field, he was a well-spoken man with dashing good looks who became a big favorite with the fans.

Although the Giants could not capture another championship, they remained one of the strongest teams in the NFL for some time. And Gifford may have been the most vital ingredient in the Giants' success formula. Between his running, receiving, and passing (he fired 14 career touchdown strikes off the halfback option), Frank was as unstoppable as any single player in the league.

"Frank Gifford," remarked one reporter, "is the kind of player who gives defenses headaches. If they stop his running, he'll hurt them with his option passing. If they stop his option passing, he'll hurt them with his receiving. But one way or another, this triple-threater will hurt them."

After running his string of Pro Bowl appearances to six in 1957–59 (he was also named Most Valuable Player of the 1959 game), Frank's superb career very nearly came to an abrupt halt late in the 1960 campaign.

The Giants were playing the Philadelphia Eagles when suddenly Gifford was smashed to the turf by a hard blindside tackle by the Eagles' fierce middle linebacker, Chuck Bednarik. Frank sustained a severe concussion.

Although team physicians gave him the go-ahead for

Gifford bursting through a hole against the Cleveland Browns.

the 1961 season, Frank decided to retire. He reasoned that he wouldn't play much longer anyway. And there was a lucrative television contract luring him to the broadcast booth.

The "retirement" lasted only one year. Still in prime physical condition at the age of 32, Frank couldn't stand to be away from football. He rejoined the Giants before the 1962 season.

Initially, things did not proceed smoothly for the returning star. Allie Sherman, the Giants' new coach, decided to use Frank as a flanker, where his sure fingers and fine moves could be employed to best advantage. Just coming back to play was difficult enough for Gifford; the position change made things that much harder on him.

"As a running back, all of Frank's moves were to the right," noted Kyle Rote, an assistant coach and close friend of Gifford's, in explaining the difficulty of the transition. "Now he has to move mostly to the left. This is like becoming a switch-hitter in baseball after swinging one way all your life."

Gifford struggled. He had trouble holding on to the ball, and the more his troubles persisted, the more his confidence tumbled. But he kept at it. He hadn't become an NFL star by quitting in the face of a challenge.

After spending the first several games on the bench, Frank caught a couple of key passes against the St. Louis Cardinals. That was all he needed. With his confidence restored, he quickly regained his star status and became one of the most-feared receivers in the league.

By season's end, Gifford had gathered 39 passes for 796 yards (a remarkable 20.4 yards per catch) and 7 touchdowns. He then added the "Comeback Player of the Year" award to his growing list of honors.

In 1963, Frank resumed his astonishing comeback in splendid fashion, catching 42 passes for 657 yards and making 7 more touchdowns. Among his catches was an acrobatic grab against the Pittsburgh Steelers that proved to be the key to an important New York victory. The Giants went on to the NFL championship game, where Frank's 14-yard touchdown reception was the Giants' only touchdown in a 14–10 loss to the Bears.

The 1964 season was Gifford's last. That year, his 29 receptions for 429 yards lifted his three-year totals in his "second career" to 110 catches for 1,184 yards and 17 touchdowns.

Overall, Gifford's career totals accurately reflected his incredible versatility on the gridiron. He picked up 9,753 total yards: 3,609 yards rushing; 5,434 yards on 367 pass receptions; 112 yards on interception returns; 118 on punt returns; and 480 on kickoff returns. His total of 78 touchdowns is one of his numerous Giant records.

Frank Gifford wasn't breathtakingly fast. He wasn't exceptionally strong, and he certainly wasn't big by football standards. What he did have was a lot of natural ability. But, more importantly, what made him such an outstanding player was that he worked hard and took his abilities as far as he possibly could. The ultimate team player, he had that rare quality that makes teams great: He was a winner.

"Frank's greatest contribution to the Giants," said Coach Sherman, "is his winning habit."

Frank Gifford had the winning habit, all right, and one way or another, the New York Giants' Mr. Versatility almost always kept it.

JIM BROWN

Sam Huff, the ferocious middle linebacker of the New York Giants, once described what it was like trying to tackle Jimmy Brown.

"All you can do," Huff said, "is grab hold, hang on, and wait for help."

In his nine record-breaking seasons as the Cleveland Browns' fullback, Brown made life miserable for NFL defenders. An awesome physical specimen at 6-foot-2 and 230 pounds, Brown had a statuesque body that provided him with a devastating combination of speed and power. A slim, 32-inch waist fit snugly between a massive torso and a pair of rippling, muscle-packed thighs.

There may never be another like him. NFL defenders certainly hope not. The typical Brown run would begin with Number 32 running *over* gigantic linemen, then running *past* fleet-footed defensive backs. "If there has ever been an unstoppable football player," a writer once remarked, "Jim Brown is him. It should be illegal to run that hard and that fast."

If Jim was unstoppable, he also was indestructible. He never missed a game in his career. That claim cannot be made by many who tried to tackle him.

Brown's road to greatness began as a schoolboy at

Manhasset High School on New York's Long Island. One look at the youngster was all the coaches needed to know they had a rare athlete on their hands. A starter on the varsity football team at the tender age of 14, Jim went on to achieve All-State honors in football, basketball, and track. As a senior, he averaged an unheard-of 15 yards per carry on the football field. He also averaged 38 points a game for Manhasset's basketball team.

That wasn't all. Jim was a standout lacrosse player, too. And, in his spare time, he managed to become so good at baseball that he later attracted offers from the New York Yankees and the Boston Braves.

It's no wonder that a former coach of Jim's once marveled, "Name the game, and he'll play it like a pro in 48 hours. He could be All-American in anything from tiddlywinks to football."

Jim's talent had no bounds. A class president and B student, he received almost 50 scholarship offers in his senior year at Manhasset. With the guidance of a close friend, Kenneth Molloy, Brown chose Syracuse University in upstate New York. Syracuse wasn't a big-time football power then. But Molloy, a graduate of the school, told Jim that Syracuse was rapidly improving its football program.

Brown's career at Syracuse started slowly. He didn't get much playing time until late in his sophomore year. Jim had his first big day in his junior year, when he rumbled for 150 yards against Cornell. But after a subpar game in his next outing, Brown was back on the "splinters." "That made me so mad I saw fire," Jim remembered. "And in the next practice scrimmage, I left first-string tacklers all over the field and ran for four touchdowns in five plays."

That performance was enough to convince the coaches

that Brown belonged in the backfield, not on the bench. Jim went on to finish second in the East in rushing yardage.

He continued to impress people as a senior, when he ran for 125 yards against Army and 145 against Maryland. Then, in his last regular-season game as a collegian, Brown broke loose. He powered for 197 yards and 6 touchdowns in a 67–6 romp over archrival Colgate. Including his 7 extra-point conversions, Brown's personal scoring total for the game was 43 points!

Still, it wasn't until Brown's final game at Syracuse that he drew the rave notices that he deserved. After losing just one game all season, the Orangemen squared off against Texas Christian in the Cotton Bowl. As a nationwide television audience looked on, Brown's star rose higher than it ever had before.

Syracuse lost, 28–27, but it was no fault of Brown's. The bruising fullback gained 132 yards and scored three touchdowns. He was named the game's most outstanding player.

A couple of months later, the news was all over the sports pages: Coach Paul Brown of the Cleveland Browns had drafted Jim Brown. This made a lot of other NFL teams green with envy. Word was out that the overpowering Syracuse product was a blue-chip pro prospect.

Almost immediately, Cleveland fans began comparing Brown to Marion Motley, the Browns' former all-star fullback. It wasn't long before the Browns had a new all-star fullback.

Forget about a year of learning. Forget about a year of adjustment. Jim Brown was plunged right into NFL battle from the start of his rookie year in 1957. He responded by leading the league in rushing with 942 yards, scoring nine touchdowns, and averaging 4.7 yards per carry. In helping the Browns capture the Eastern Conference crown, Jim was a runaway choice for Rookie of the Year. Along the way, the awesome powerhouse also set a new NFL record by rushing for 237 yards against the Los Angeles Rams. It took him only a year to be hailed as the NFL's best running back.

"Brown really shivers you," said Matt Hazeltine, a linebacker with the San Francisco 49'ers. "I wonder how many KO's he would've scored when there were no face masks."

Jim's second season with the Browns was even greater. Not only did he lead the NFL in rushing again with a league-record 1,527 yards, he also led in scoring, with 18 touchdowns for 106 points. He averaged an amazing 5.9 yards every time he carried the ball. Although only in his second year as a pro, Brown was in a class by himself. No matter how much defenses keyed on him, Brown simply could not be stopped. Trying to tackle him one-on-one was usually futile—and always dangerous. Even gang-tackling often couldn't stop his furious charges.

Brown's career continued on its same spectacular course. In a game against the NFL-champion Baltimore Colts in 1959, Brown blasted for five touchdowns to spark a stunning, 38–31 upset.

If his individual performances were dramatic, the annual derbies for the rushing title were not. Brown took all the mystery out of it. The NFL record book tells the story:

Rushing Leaders

1959—Jim Brown, 1,329 yards
1960—Jim Brown, 1,257 yards
1961—Jim Brown, 1,408 yards

In his first five seasons, Jim Brown led the NFL in rushing five times. That's a tough act to follow. It's highly unlikely that any back will ever do that again.

The unprecedented streak *had* to stop sometime—and 1962 was the year. Brown had an "off" year, gaining a mere 996 yards and scoring 13 touchdowns. Jim Taylor of the Packers became the first runner since 1957 to beat Brown for the rushing crown.

But Brown had spoiled the Cleveland fans, who expected him to be *the* best every year. "I'm no Superman," he said. "I had a good season—not a great one, though. Do I have to lead the league *every* time for it to be a good year? I don't like to boast, but I think I'm as good as anyone in this league as an all-around offensive player."

That was a gross understatement. And he proved it in 1963, when he abruptly silenced his critics by having the greatest year a running back had ever had. Named the NFL Player of the Year, Brown broke his own single-season rushing mark by rolling up an incredible 1,863 yards. He averaged 6.4 yards per carry and scored 12 touchdowns.

Brown also single-handedly won one of Cleveland's biggest games of the year. With the Browns trailing the New York Giants, the defending Eastern Conference champions, 27–14, Jim went to work. Taking a screen pass, he barreled through heavy traffic and sprinted 72 yards for a touchdown. Then, late in the game, he burst right up the middle for the game-winner—a 32-yard touchdown.

Some teams tried anything they could to stop the Browns' punishing powerhouse. In one game, Jim recalled plowing through the line when suddenly he felt a hand inside his face mask, trying to poke his eyes. "Once I

"I'm no Superman," said Brown once. NFL defenders weren't so sure.

felt him clawing for my eyes," said Jim later, "I got my teeth into that hand. I'll bet it hasn't run under any more masks since then."

Jim chewed up the league's defenses some more in 1964. He amassed 1,446 yards for the rushing title to lead the Browns to a conference crown. Then, against the heavily favored Colts in the NFL championship game, Cleveland coasted to a 27–0 victory. Jim didn't score any touchdowns, but he did rush for 114 yards and had a big effect on the outcome. The Colt defense was so intent on stopping Brown that Cleveland quarterback Frank Ryan had a field day in the air, passing for three touchdowns.

Jim retired after the 1965 season. He always said he wanted to leave the game at his peak, and that's just what he did. In his ninth, and last, season, Brown led the NFL ground gainers with 1,544 yards, his eighth rushing title in his brilliant nine-year career. No other player has ever led the league in rushing more than four times.

Brown left the game with virtually every NFL rushing record in his pocket. O. J. Simpson has since surpassed some of them, but many of Brown's marks remain intact, including: most rushing yards gained, career, 12,312; most touchdowns, career, 126; most seasons leading league in rushing, 8; most seasons, 1,000 or more yards rushing, 7; most games, 100 or more yards rushing, career, 58; most rushing attempts, career, 2,358; and highest gain per carry, career, 5.22 yards.

Brown and Simpson have often been compared. But, in a sense, it's like comparing apples and oranges. Jim was a fullback; O. J. is a halfback. O. J. is faster and a bit more elusive; Jim was stronger and more punishing. O. J. has a completely different style. He's more of a slasher, a nimble-footed speedster who slides and jukes and spurts

Number 32—he had the power to run through them and the speed to run by them.

through holes with uncanny swiftness. Brown was more of a bruiser, an awesome force who often made his own holes before streaking away with astonishing speed and agility.

The comparisons will undoubtedly continue, but most NFL observers agree on this much: Brown was the greatest fullback ever to play, and Simpson is the greatest halfback ever to play.

In any case, Brown has never been the type of man to recite his records and call himself the best. "I never dwell on what I did," Jim said. "That's history. I have a lot of pleasant memories of a game that was a good part of my life."

He continued, "I think every record I've ever made will get wiped out, ultimately. Always, you're going to have to have guys coming along and improving. That's great—the way it needs to be, because that's progress, that's advancement."

There's another, far more important kind of advancement Jim has been concerned with—the advancement of black people. Brown enlisted scores of well-known athletes to assist him in forming a group designed to help blacks achieve economic equality.

After his playing days, Jim also embarked on a career in motion pictures. He has appeared in *The Dirty Dozen* and *Rio Concho,* among other films.

But Jim Brown will always be remembered best as fearsome Number 32 of the Cleveland Browns, a number that terrorized NFL defenders for nine seasons. With good reason, they dreaded the sight of him carrying the ball. There has never been a mightier force on the football field than Jim Brown, the most prolific ground-gainer in NFL history.

It wasn't until late in Brown's career that anybody figured out a way to stop him. The idea came from Alex Karras, a defensive tackle with the Detroit Lions and long-time foe of Brown's. Alex's idea?

"Give everybody in the line an ax."

GALE SAYERS

Gale Sayers made his mark in the NFL the same way he ran with the football—in a hurry. The sad thing was that it had to be that way. After less than five full seasons, two crippling knee injuries all but ended the brilliant career of a man who, despite his short tenure, was voted the best halfback of the NFL's first 50 years.

Three separate times, Sayers pushed and punished himself with a long, arduous rehabilitation program. But it was futile. The most-feared legs in the NFL were irreparably damaged. Never again would he thrill NFL fans with the blinding, breathtaking dashes that made him perhaps the most dazzling runner in league history.

Short career or not, Gale Sayers was the rare kind of player you could not forget. In 1977, his first year of eligibility, he was unanimously elected to the Pro Football Hall of Fame. "There never was another to compare with him," praised the voting committee. "What else is there to say?"

From the moment Gale joined the Chicago Bears in 1965, Coach George Halas knew he had someone special. But not even the venerable Halas, the founder and owner of the Bears, knew just *how* special Gale would be.

A first-round draft choice from the University of Kansas, Sayers had compiled a stunning collegiate record. "The Kansas Comet," they called him, and with good reason. The 6-foot, 200-pound All-American rushed for 2,675 yards and tacked on over 1,200 more on pass receptions and kick returns.

Electing to bring his prize rookie along slowly, Halas didn't start Sayers until the third game of the 1965 season. Gale's impact was immediate. Although the Bears lost to the Green Bay Packers, 23–14, Sayers was outstanding. He scored both Chicago touchdowns, the first on a 6-yard burst off-tackle and the second on an electrifying 65-yard pass play. His performance prompted one reporter to write, "Gale Sayers has burst from his rookie cocoon and come alive."

As great as Gale's debut was, it was a mere glimpse of the greatness that was to come. Against the Los Angeles Rams the following week, Sayers scampered 80 yards with a screen pass. He reversed his role later in the contest, throwing—not catching—a 26-yard touchdown on an option pass.

Some skeptics questioned whether Sayers was strong enough to withstand the rigors of the pro game. Anyone with doubts about Sayers could have asked Rosey Grier, the Rams' massive, 300-pound tackle. Grier thought he had nailed Sayers but good on Gale's 80-yard touchdown. "I hit him so hard, I thought my shoulder must have busted him in two," Grier commented later. "I heard a roar from the crowd and figured he had fumbled. So I started scrambling around looking for the loose ball. But there was no ball and Sayers was long gone."

The Bears destroyed the Rams, 31–6. Suddenly, Sayers was the talk of the NFL. At least the talk of most of the NFL. There was one man, Minnesota Vikings' Coach Norm Van Brocklin, who apparently wasn't convinced the "Kansas Comet" was for real. Maybe it was just a "psych job," but Van Brocklin was quoted as saying that Sayers was just another fast scatback who hadn't really been hit yet.

Gale didn't have to wait long to prove Van Brocklin wrong. The Bears' next game was against the Vikings. Neither Sayers nor Van Brocklin would forget that game for a long time.

After being held in check in the first half, Sayers ran wild in the second. He scored 2 touchdowns on passes of 18 and 25 yards to help give the Bears a 31–30 lead late in the game. Then the Vikings battled back to recapture the lead, 37–30.

Sayers received the ensuing kickoff on the Chicago 4-yard line. Streaking upfield on the left side, Sayers picked up a couple of key blocks, slithered through a hole, and then simply turned on the jets. Nobody came close to him. A 9.7 sprinter is pretty tough to catch.

"It was the fastest I've ever seen a guy run through a hole," said Viking linebacker Lonnie Warwick dejectedly. "I was trying to break their blocking wedge, when suddenly Sayers cut to my right. He really turned it on, and he was past me in a second."

Sayers clinched the victory just minutes later. Taking a handoff, he powered right up the middle for an 11-yard touchdown, his fourth of the game. "I didn't go like a scatback on that one," said Gale later.

Sayers continued to tear up the league the rest of the season. In leading the Bears on a streak of 9 victories in 10 games, Sayers dazzled one opponent after another. He returned a punt 62 yards for a touchdown against the Packers; he galloped for 2 touchdowns and 113 yards (his first 100-yard day as a pro) in only 13 carries against the

An inch of daylight...and Sayers is gone.

New York Giants; and he riddled the Baltimore Colts for 118 yards, 61 of them coming on a blazing burst for a touchdown.

Going into the next-to-last game of the season, Sayers, with 15 touchdowns, had already established a new record for rookies. The night before the game, Buddy Young, a former great NFL running back and a friend of Gale's, called the star rookie. "You got a shot at Rookie of the Year, Gale," Buddy said, "but they're pushing Bob Hayes and Tucker Fredrickson. You have to have a good day against San Francisco."

"I'll see what I can do for you," replied Gale, never known as a big talker.

On a muddy, rain-soaked field—hardly a good track for a darting sprinter—all Gale did was score 6 touchdowns! His incredible performance tied a long-standing NFL record. What's more, Gale might've had a seventh touchdown if Halas, not wanting to risk an injury to his star, had not taken him out in the final minutes.

Gale's touchdown parade began on the Bears' first possession. He took a screen pass, sidestepped through heavy traffic, shook off a couple of tackles, and cruised 80 yards to the end zone. Then came touchdown rushes of 21, 7, 50, and 1 yards, before he concluded his one-man assault with a miraculous 85-yard punt return. Sayers's efforts accounted for the stunning total of 336 yards, as the Bears routed the San Francisco 49'ers, 61–20.

"That was the greatest performance I have ever seen on a football field," raved Coach Halas, who had been in the game almost 50 seasons.

That night, Gale got another call from Buddy Young. "I wanted you to have a good day," said Buddy, laughing, "but that was ridiculous."

With Rookie-of-the-Year honors now in the bag, Gale

went on to score another six-pointer in the season finale. That brought his total to 22, a new NFL record! He had even surpassed the great Jimmy Brown, who finished the year with 21 touchdowns.

Gale wound up his phenomenal rookie year, often called the greatest ever for a first-year running back, with 2,272 total yards. Of these, 862 came on the ground, for an outstanding 5.2 yards per carry. Only Brown amassed more rushing yardage that year.

Not surprisingly, Sayers's all-around brilliance turned around the entire Chicago team. Without him, in 1964, the Bears finished 5–9. With him, in 1965, they climbed to 9–5. In a single, record-shattering season, the incomparable Number 40 had become the most dangerous scoring machine in the NFL.

A rookie year like Sayers had is a tough act to follow. The second time around, Gale knew teams would gear their whole defensive strategy to try to stop him. Easier said than done.

There was simply no stopping Sayers. His second season was even better than his first. The Bears had a disappointing year, but Sayers was anything but disappointing.

Thanks to a glittering, 197-yard rushing performance in a victory over the Vikings in the final game of the year, Gale passed Leroy Kelly of the Browns for the NFL rushing title. Sayers's total was 1,231 yards on 229 carries, good for 5.4 yards per carry.

But that was hardly all. Sayers set a new NFL record with 2,440 total yards, and also led the league in kickoff returns with a 31.2-yard average and 2 touchdowns. He racked up four 100-yard outings, including 172 against the Atlanta Falcons and the 197 against the Vikings. To cap it all off, for the second straight year Sayers was named to the Pro Bowl, where he walked off with Offensive-Player-of-the-Game honors.

By Sayers's lofty standards, 1967 was an off year. After a slow start for both him and his team, Gale suffered a nagging foot injury and a stomach disorder. He lost 25 pounds because of the stomach problem, and late in the year, he was still well off the pace in the rushing title.

But Gale shrugged it off, charging back in typical fashion. He gained more than 100 yards in three of his last four games, finishing the campaign with 880 yards on the ground for third place in the NFL.

It was another sensational season for Sayers, the kick-return specialist. Averaging almost 38 yards a crack, Gale streaked for three touchdowns, two of them for 97 yards. The third touchdown, which came in the opening game, went for 103 yards, among the longest returns in NFL history.

Those three lifted his career touchdown total on kickoff returns to six, an NFL record that stands to this day.

Gale finished the year in style, again being named Offensive Player of the Game in the Pro Bowl. Still, Sayers maintained that 1967 was an off year. You can bet dozens of backs throughout the NFL would have dearly loved to have such an "off year."

Determined to have his greatest year ever in 1968, Sayers got off to a sizzling start. He was devastating. By mid-season, he already had posted four 100-yard games. And in the finest rushing game of his career, he bolted for 205 yards against the Packers. His totals for eight games were remarkable: 856 yards rushing, 6.2 yards per carry, 603 yards in kickoff returns, and almost 1,700 yards overall. He was headed for one of the best years in NFL history.

And then it happened. In the ninth game of the year, Gale was skirting right end against the 49'ers, when he was hit with a crunching tackle. His right knee buckled, suffering extensive ligament damage. For Sayers, the season was over. That right knee would never be the same again.

After working tirelessly to rebuild the knee in the off-season, Gale pronounced himself ready to play in 1969. Was he ever! After a sluggish start, he staged a dramatic late-season resurgence to capture his second NFL rushing crown. And he did it while playing on a team with the worst record in the league.

Gale's performance far transcended his statistics, which included 1,032 yards rushing and 8 touchdowns. Voted the NFL's "Comeback Player of the Year," he had won the admiration of football fans all over the country.

It's the ultimate tribute to Gale's talent and courage that he won the rushing title in 1969. He just was not the same Gale Sayers, the man who, prior to the injury, could break for a touchdown from anywhere on the field. In the *Chicago Daily News,* a reporter commented, "Gone are that instant acceleration from medium to top speed and the incomparable ability to change directions on a dime without hesitation or loss of speed."

Gale Sayers was not the same. But he still was the best. He had great expectations for another league-leading season in 1970 . . . until disaster struck again. Returning a kick in a preseason game against the St. Louis Cardinals, Gale was smacked by a Cardinal rookie. This time it was the left knee that was ravaged.

He desperately wanted to wait until the end of the season for an operation. But after two games, it was painfully apparent that the old magic wasn't there. He underwent two operations, then tested his knee again in

End zone-bound against the Los Angeles Rams.

1971. After playing in two games, he knew his knee hadn't recovered.

Gale made his one last comeback bid in 1972. To no avail. The career of one of the greatest running backs of all time came to a sad end during that preseason.

The legacy of his brilliant, abbreviated career is an amazing array of statistics: 9,435 total yards; 4,956 yards rushing; 336 total points; 5.0 yards per carry; 22 touchdowns in one season; and 6 touchdowns in one game.

As impressive as these numbers are, there's no telling how much greater they could have been. His career was over at 28. For Gale Sayers, it had ended much too soon.

DICK BUTKUS

With two back-to-back selections in the first round of the 1965 NFL college draft, owner-coach George Halas of the Chicago Bears picked himself an offense and a defense...a game-breaker and a body-breaker.

The offense was Gale Sayers. The defense was Dick Butkus. No team has ever improved itself so much with just two draft picks. And probably no team ever will.

Sayers's breathtaking brilliance instantly made him the most dangerous runner in the league. Butkus? At 6-foot-3 and 245 pounds, he wasn't going to dazzle people the way Sayers did. Nor was he supposed to. His job, as middle linebacker, was to anchor the defense. And he did it better than any middle linebacker in NFL history.

In only one season, Butkus transformed the league's second *worst* defense into the league's second best defense. "Dick Butkus," wrote one reporter, "*is* the Chicago Bears' defense." True enough. And he remained the Chicago Bears' defense until 1973, when a string of serious injuries finally caught up with him and ended his unmatched career.

"When Butkus retired," said Mick Tingelhoff, the Minnesota Vikings' perennial all-pro center, "it added three years to my career."

From the start, there was never a doubt that Butkus was something special. "The day Dick showed up," said

Bill George, the man Butkus replaced in the Chicago middle, "I knew I was out of a job."

Strong, smart, and quick, Butkus was ideally suited to the post that one former NFL coach described as "the toughest position to play well." He immediately earned the reputation as the meanest, most ferocious defender in the game. Dick Butkus. Even the name sounds mean.

"There are guys who make tackles and then there's Dick," observed Doug Buffone, a Bears' linebacker who played alongside Butkus. "He's a mauler. I hit pretty hard, but no matter how hard I hit, I don't hit that hard."

Fran Tarkenton, who had more than his share of run-ins with Butkus during his career, agreed. "You just can't believe a guy hits that hard. You just can't seem to fool him away from a play either . . . I think Dick Butkus is the greatest football player I've ever seen. Certainly the toughest."

In his book, *Tarkenton,* Francis praised Butkus this way: "He was so great he could take a group of average football players around him and make them play better than they knew how to play because they respected him so much they were scared of what he would do to them if they didn't play.

"Whenever you played the Chicago Bears you were aware of Dick Butkus . . . You were aware of Butkus because you knew that any time you ran or passed successfully you would somehow have to escape him. He was going to make an interception or he was going to chase a play forty yards . . . He kept his team in a frenzy every game. He was the most dominating single player I've ever seen in a football defense. He had the kind of temperament that made him want to engulf the whole offense by himself." And he often did.

The nasty nemesis: Dick Butkus.

"King Kong." "Gorilla." "Subhuman." "Animal." Those are just a few of the words used by the opposing players Butkus battered during his career. None of them faze Dick in the least.

"I play the game the way I think it should be played," he remarked once. "And if they think that animalistic, well . . . Still in all, I must be doing something for them to be calling me names. It doesn't bother me."

Being rugged came naturally to Dick, who grew up with his eight brothers and sisters in a tough neighborhood in Chicago. He started playing the game early in that football-crazy town. It soon became his calling.

"In the fifth grade," says Dick, "I knew what I was going to be—a professional football player. I worked hard at becoming one, just like society says you should. It said you had to be fierce. I was fierce. Tough. I was tough."

Butkus was fierce and tough enough to win a scholarship to the University of Illinois, where he was a two-time All-American, first as a center, then as a linebacker.

When Butkus first joined the Bears, some NFL quarterbacks thought that the burly linebacker wasn't quick enough to defend against the pass. They figured a man that big simply couldn't be too effective on pass coverage. They were wrong—and they found out quickly.

"I once looked him off a pass," recalled Norm Snead, then a quarterback for the New York Giants. "I faked and faked, and he kept sliding over and over to where I was looking. Then I suddenly turned and threw to the other side of the field. That man was there to knock the ball down, and I think it was a time when his leg was bothering him, too."

44

Butkus intercepted five passes his rookie season. That's hardly the mark of a slow man.

"I've never been timed in a 40-yard dash, and I could care less," Dick said once. "They always said I was weak on passes because I was the biggest and weighed the most...I wonder if I got down to 235 and was the same weight as others, if they would say the same thing."

"He looks fat, clumsy, and awkward," said Tommy Prothro, former coach of the Los Angeles Rams and San Diego Chargers, "but he kicks the devil out of everybody. And if you pass, he's there too."

Whatever Butkus lacked in foot speed, he more than compensated for it with intelligence and an uncanny ability to read plays. "Butkus has to be the smartest middle linebacker I've ever seen," said Abe Gibron, Dick's last pro coach and a man who has been around the NFL for more than a quarter of a century.

Butkus worked tirelessly—mentally and physically— to develop his anticipation and knowledge of the game. "The first couple of years," he commented, "I played on physical ability alone. As the years go by, you learn what experience means, just watching a team and knowing what they'll go to, being able to read patterns, knowing where to go yourself."

He went on to describe what Tarkenton once termed his "technical brilliance."

"At the key moment, the instant of the snap, I somehow know most of the time how the flow pattern will develop. It's all there in the backdrop. I stare right through the center and the quarterback, right through their eyes.

"I watch for the keys, and they are very tiny keys. Tiny little twitches of the shoulders, and their heads and their feet and eyes. There's just this split second, before it all

45

starts to move, when you put those keys together and you know—or you better—how it's going."

It's that kind of mental work, along with his fierce intensity and relentless hustle, that enabled Butkus seemingly to be in the middle of every play. Many quarterbacks have said that Butkus was the hardest linebacker in the league to fool.

If Butkus had a superb knack for sniffing out plays, he also had a superb nose for the ball. He recovered 7 fumbles in his first season, and by the time he retired, he had set a new NFL record with 25 fumble recoveries. And that doesn't include countless other fumbles, pounced on by his teammates, which were caused by a typical bone-crunching Butkus tackle.

But no matter how many interceptions Butkus made or how many fumbles he recovered, he was the kind of player whose dominance went far beyond the statistics sheet. Even the number of tackles he made in a given game often would not reveal how brilliantly he had played. Intimidation simply can't be measured by numbers. Nor can the way he altered a quarterback's game plan be measured. That's what Butkus was best at—unsettling an offense, making it play into his hands.

"The best kind of defense," Butkus has said, "is the kind that forces the offense to react." In other words, the defense dictates to the offense.

An all-pro in each of his eight complete seasons, Butkus was honored by his fellow players as the NFL's outstanding defender in 1969 and again in 1970, despite a knee injury that hampered him much of the year.

Butkus underwent surgery following the 1970 season, and there was some doubt about whether he would still be the best middle linebacker in the game. One reporter predicted that Baltimore's Mike Curtis would surpass Butkus as the best and meanest man in the middle. Dick did not react kindly to that notion.

"When I saw that story," he related, "I sat down and had a long talk with my knee. I told my knee all about it. All during camp, whenever I felt like taking it easy, I'd remind my knee of Curtis."

Any doubt about Dick's status atop the league's linebackers was summarily crunched to the ground—along with a number of Pittsburgh Steelers—in his first preseason game. The Steelers tested the Chicago iron man on their second play, when John Fuqua barreled up the middle, right into Butkus's territory. Wham! Butkus smacked into Fuqua head on, hurling the back to the ground. Dick played like a man possessed that game—as he did in most. He made seven unassisted tackles, picked off two passes, caused a fumble that led to the Bears' game-winning tally, and generally created havoc among the Pittsburgh offensive ranks.

No linebacker could create havoc—and instill fear—like Butkus. Butkus's teammate, the late Brian Piccolo, once described how he felt playing against him: "When Dick is on the other side of the scrimmage line, glaring at you with those boiling eyes, it makes you wish you could change places with the equipment boy."

Two more knee operations after the 1971 season didn't stop Butkus from having another all-pro year in 1972. One of his most memorable games that year came against the Vikings in a Monday-night contest. In addition to his normal defensive work—five tackles, a fumble recovery, and an interception—Butkus keyed a Chicago victory with a couple of ingenious play calls in kicking situations. With Butkus providing the tip, the Bear quarterback faked a field goal attempt and ran for a first down. Later, on another suggestion from Dick, the Bears faked a punt and passed 23 yards for a first down.

"The Vikings have a great kick rush," Butkus explained later. "I studied their films all week." So Butkus came up with the trick plays to take advantage of the Vikings' over-eager charge.

Butkus was a winner, but perhaps the greatest enduring frustration of his tremendous career was that the Bears were not. Only twice in the Butkus years did the Bears finish over .500. Dick had his own way of coping with losing. He once explained his pregame routine: "I look over at the other team warming up, and I look for guys who are smiling or fooling around or acting silly. Then I say to myself, 'He thinks he's going to have it easy today, huh? That sets me off, and the more I watch, the hotter I get. When the game starts, I'm ready to tear people apart."

It was that kind of competitiveness and almost manic intensity that put Dick Butkus in a class by himself. "I have never seen a player with greater desire," said his coach, Abe Gibron. "He's a once-in-a-generation ballplayer."

"Dick Butkus," agreed Tommy Prothro, "is a legendary football player."

"Every time I play a game," Dick said late in his career, "I want to play it like it was my last one. I could get hurt, and that would be it for keeps. I wouldn't want my last game to be a lousy one."

There's no question that Dick Butkus was a driven man—driven by an overpowering, unrelenting desire. "My goal," he said once, "is to be recognized as the best. When they say middle linebacker, I want them to mean Butkus."

Dick Butkus attained that goal. Because to this day, when people say middle linebacker, they "mean Butkus."

"When they say middle linebacker," said Dick, "I want them to mean Butkus."

BART STARR

Just 16 seconds remained in the 1967 NFL championship game. Trailing the Dallas Cowboys, 17–14, the Green Bay Packers had the ball inside the Dallas one-yard line.

The frigid crowd at Lambeau Field in Green Bay, Wisconsin, stood in silent, frozen anticipation. The biting, 15-degrees-below-zero cold had, for the moment, drifted into the background. All that mattered was whether the Pack could score a touchdown and become the first team in NFL history to win three consecutive championships.

The Packers had used their last time-out. It was third down. A pass would be too risky. A game-tying field goal was out of the question. "If we can't get the ball into the end zone," snapped Green Bay Coach Vince Lombardi to his quarterback, Bart Starr, "we don't deserve to be NFL champions." The Packers had to run. It would be their last play of the game.

Footing on the tundra-like field was next to impossible. Linemen couldn't dig in; runners couldn't cut. The Pack's last two cracks at the rugged Dallas line had resulted in no gain.

Starr calmly huddled with his team. The quarterback made his call; the determined Packers broke their huddle. The championship had come down to a single play. The two great teams lined up, nose to nose, steamy clouds of anxious breath hovering in the icy air over every poised body.

"Hut! Hut!" barked Starr. Bodies crunched and clashed. Forrest Gregg and Jerry Kramer charged. The great Packer linemen hit low and hard. Starr slithered behind them. He darted into the end zone. Touchdown! The Packers had done it!

Thawing with relief and jubilation, the crowd went wild. The Packers mobbed their quarterback. The normally quiet, unemotional Starr was overcome with joy. This was too much. He fought back tears as he left the field.

That championship-winning quarterback sneak was vintage Bart Starr: simple, unspectacular—but overwhelmingly successful.

There have been more flamboyant and widely publicized quarterbacks in NFL history. There have been quarterbacks with more impressive statistics.

But there have been few, if any, quarterbacks more effective—or, for that matter, more intelligent—than Bryan Bartlett Starr. Winning is the bottom line in pro football. And there has never been a quarterback who won as consistently as Starr did in the Packers glory years in the 1960s.

In his placid, low-key way, Starr guided the Pack to an amazing record of 82-24-4 from 1960 through 1967. More importantly, in that span the Packers captured six divisional titles, five NFL titles, and the first two Super Bowls. Starr was named Most Valuable Player in each of the Pack's Super Bowl triumphs.

Some people have argued that those Packer teams were so great that they could have won with even a run-of-the-mill quarterback. But knowledgeable football people will tell you that simply isn't so. Coach Lombardi himself, never one to heap excessive praise on his players, acknowledged that a quarterback means "everything" to a team, no matter how great it is.

"He's the perfect quarterback for the team he is with," observed former New York Giants' Coach Allie Sherman of Starr. "He rarely makes mistakes."

"Bart Starr has better timing on calling plays and taking advantage of the defenses than anyone I have ever seen," said former San Francisco 49'ers Coach Jack Christianson. "Someday he may be recognized as the greatest ever."

Indeed, Bart fashioned his brilliant career around that very point—minimizing mistakes. Starr once explained his philosophy. "As long as we have the ball, they [the other team] can't hurt us with it. You can see what an interception can do to a drive, so we do everything we can to avoid mistakes. It's foolish to take chances when possession is so important."

That philosophy was a vital ingredient of the Packers' success. With Starr at the helm, the Packers were very stingy with their turnovers. At one point in his career, Bart threw 294 passes without an interception! That's one NFL record many experts believe will never be broken.

In 1966, when Bart led the NFL in passing for the third time (he also did it in 1962 and 1964), he threw only 3 interceptions in 251 passes. Furthermore, in his six appearances in championship games, only one of his 142 attempts was picked off.

The all-time NFL leader in completion percentage—he connected on more than 57 percent of his aerials—Bart always seemed to be at his deadliest when it counted the most. In a thrilling 34–27 victory over Dallas in the 1966 NFL championship match, Starr gunned for 304 yards

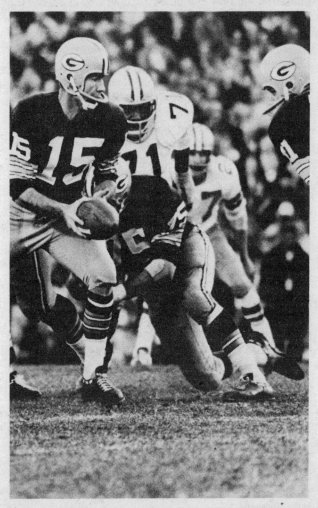

Bart hands off to hard-running fullback, Jim Taylor.

and 4 touchdowns on 19-of-28 passing. His performance paced the Packers to a place in Super Bowl I against the Kansas City Chiefs of the AFL. Bart was every bit as good in that game, completing 16 of 23 passes for 250 yards, 2 touchdowns, a 35–10 blowout, and Most Valuable Player trophy.

Before his historic, last-second plunge into the end zone in the 1967 NFL title game, Starr had riddled the Cowboys with two clutch touchdown passes. Then, in Super Bowl II, he picked apart the Oakland Raiders with the same uncanny precision he had shown against the Chiefs. He connected on 13 of his 24 passes for 202 yards and a touchdown. The Pack romped again, 33–14.

Earlier in that contest, Starr showed why he was perhaps the most astute play-caller in football. In a third-and-one situation from the Green Bay 38-yard line, Starr noticed that the Oakland defense was bunched in close for the expected running play. Then, the master of surprise faked a handoff, caught the Raiders off-guard, and lofted a 62-yard scoring strike to receiver Boyd Dowler.

One of the quickest-thinking quarterbacks who ever played, Starr was famous for calling audibles—changing the play at the line of scrimmage. He could size up defenses instantly, then coolly shift his strategy to take advantage of weaknesses that he detected.

Bart's intelligence was one of the first things Packer Coach Lisle Blackbourn noticed when Starr was a rookie in 1956. But the coach wasn't overly impressed with anything else about the rookie. "You have a quick way of understanding offenses and defenses," Blackbourn told Starr. "But I think you would make a better teacher of quarterbacks. You're going to have a tough time making it in the pros."

Bart respectfully disagreed. "I'm going to try to make it as a pro quarterback," he responded quietly.

But even Bart himself wasn't sure if he could make the grade. A lowly, 17th-round draft choice from the University of Alabama, Bart wasn't exactly brimming over with confidence when he reported to the Packers.

He had shown a lot of promise in his first two years at Alabama, when he led the Crimson Tide to a 61–6 rout of Syracuse in the Cotton Bowl. But things went steadily downhill for him after that. He was plagued by injuries in his junior year. Then, in his senior year, he rode the bench.

Bart managed to stick with the Packers, but he was strictly a part-timer his first several seasons. Every year he had to struggle just to make the team, at that time, one of the weakest in the NFL. Neither Starr nor the Packers seemed to be going anywhere.

He had his first big day as a professional in 1958. In a losing cause against the Baltimore Colts, the young quarterback completed 26 of 46 passes for 320 yards. But Bart, sorely lacking in confidence, was erratic. And none of the Packer coaches seemed to think he was the answer to the club's persistent quarterback problems.

Starr continued to struggle in 1959, the year Lombardi took over the team. That coach-quarterback combination would eventually mold the Pack into the greatest dynasty in NFL history. But then, although Lombardi thought Starr had potential, the coach looked elsewhere for an experienced quarterback. He traded for veteran Lamar McHan.

"I don't blame Coach Lombardi for trading for Lamar," said Bart softly when the deal was announced. "The Packers do need a quarterback. I haven't been doing the job. And now it looks like I never will."

Bart's confidence had plummeted even lower by the sixth game of the season. With McHan injured, Lombardi elected to go with tailback Joe Francis as his quarterback. Starr was passed over. The Packers lost the game, 20–3. The next time Lombardi wanted a quarterback, he went to Starr.

With the team wallowing under .500, the coach gave Bart a shot at the starting job late in the season. Starr responded by winning four straight games. While impressing the coach with his intelligence and leadership, Bart threw for 699 yards on deadly 52-of-79 passing.

Led by Starr, the Packers' late-season resurgence enabled them to finish over .500 (7–5) for the first time in 12 years. Bart Starr had a job. The Green Bay Packers had a quarterback. And the success stories of the quarterback, the coach, and the team were just beginning. "I owe my football life to Lombardi," Bart commented later. "He developed me, motivated me, stayed with me, built my confidence."

In his first full season as the Packers' number-one quarterback, Starr guided his team to the NFL's Western Conference title in 1960. The parade of championships began the following year, when the Packers walloped the New York Giants, 37–0, in the title game.

The Packers repeated in 1962, as Starr led the NFL in passing. The quarterback completed 178 of his 285 passes for an incredible 62.5 percentage.

Although the Packers continued to rack up title after title, Starr didn't receive much acclaim. That was reserved for the Pack's superb backfield tandem of Jim Taylor and Paul Hornung—and for Lombardi himself.

The lack of attention didn't faze Bart in the least. In keeping with his quiet nature, he was perfectly content to let others grab the headlines, so long as the Packers

Smiling Coach Starr: Bringing winning football to Green Bay.

continued to grab the championships. And that's what the Packers did, right up through 1967, the year Lombardi retired. After that, the years gradually crept up on the aging Pack. Piece by piece, the great Packer machine came apart.

Perhaps the most indispensable part of that machine, Bart Starr, continued to stand out for the Pack until his retirement before the 1972 season.

His 16-year statistics reflected an outstanding career: 3,149 attempts; 1,808 completions; 57.4 completion percentage; 24,688 passing yards; and 152 touchdowns.

But for Bart Starr, who hardly gave a thought to personal records and accomplishments, the statistics don't begin to tell the story.

This is what tells the story for Bart Starr—six divisional titles; five NFL championships; and two Super Bowl championships. The bottom line.

"Bart Starr," noted one long-time Packer follower, "was a winner."

JOHNNY UNITAS

This story is a fairy tale. There's no other way to describe it.

It's a vintage rags-to-riches tale that shows just how far hard work and determination can take a talented person. The hero of the story is John Unitas, who emerged from the obscurity of sandlot football to become the player voted the greatest quarterback in the NFL's first 50 years.

The year was 1955. An unheralded rookie—a ninth-round draft choice out of the University of Louisville—reported to the Pittsburgh Steelers' training camp. The 22-year-old homegrown quarterback from the Brookline section of Pittsburgh had established 15 passing records at Louisville. But not many people noticed; the Kentucky school has never been known as a football powerhouse.

Still, John Unitas hoped he would get a chance to show the Steelers what he could do. The chance never came. Without getting in for even one play during the preseason games, Unitas was sent packing. All he had to show for the tryout, if it can be called that, was $10 in bus fare. "The grim thing about it," Unitas observed later, "was that the Steelers never gave me the opportunity to play."

Disappointed, John went back to Pittsburgh, where he got a construction job. But he wasn't about to abandon football, the game he had loved ever since he was a small boy. In his spare time, John played with the Bloomfield Rams of the Greater Pittsburgh League.

It was about as far from the NFL as a player could get. Playing on dusty, rock-ridden fields, Unitas drew his first wages as a football player—$3 per game. But the paltry salary didn't much matter to Unitas, who wanted to stay in shape in the hope that he would get another call from the NFL. "I would've played for nothing," stated John flatly. And he practically did, though not for long.

In February 1956, John got the call he'd been hoping for. It was from Don Kellett, general manager of the Baltimore Colts. Browsing for a quarterback through an old NFL waiver list, Kellett came across Unitas's name. Kellett consulted the Colts' coach, Weeb Ewbank, who had heard good things about Unitas from the coach at Louisville, Frank Camp. Then the general manager invited John to try out for the team.

This time, Unitas got a chance to show his stuff. And this time, he made the grade. After an impressive preseason, John was rewarded with a $7,000 contract. It didn't make him a millionaire, but it was a whole lot better than $3 a game.

John started the season as the backup quarterback. George Shaw was the starter. But when Shaw was racked up by the Chicago Bears in the fourth game of the year, Unitas was pressed into action. His debut was hardly a great one.

His first NFL pass resulted in a touchdown—for the Bears. Chicago's J. C. Caroline intercepted the young quarterback's aerial and returned it for a score. It was the start of a miserable afternoon for Unitas. Lacking game experience, unfamiliar with his new teammates, John fumbled once himself and twice more on attempted handoffs. The Colts were trounced, 56–27. It wasn't much consolation to Unitas that he threw his first touchdown pass, a 36-yarder to split end Jim Mutscheller.

John knew he wouldn't be a starting quarterback for very long if he had many more performances like that one. But he shrugged it off. Next week, against the Green Bay Packers, Unitas threw 2 touchdown passes to lead the Colts to a 28–21 triumph. After that, he engineered a 21–7 upset over the Cleveland Browns.

Unitas still had a lot to learn about playing quarterback, a position many experts believe takes five years of pro experience to master. But he worked hard, and by the end of the year, he had impressed many people, not only with his accurate passing, but with his intelligent play-calling as well.

A young team with a bright future, the Colts finished the 1956 season with a 5–7 record. No one on the team had a brighter future than Number 19, John Unitas. The 6-foot-1, 190 pounder set a new NFL record for completion percentage for rookies—55.6. He was on his way.

With a year of valuable experience behind him, Unitas was brilliant in 1957. He led the league with 2,550 yards passing, fired 24 touchdown passes (at least one in every game), and completed 172 of his 301 passes for a superb 57.1 percentage. More importantly, he led the Colts into first place in their division late in the season.

But the young Baltimore team was unable to hang on. Despite Unitas's finest performance of the season—23 completions in 37 attempts for 296 yards—the Colts dropped a 17–13 decision to San Francisco. Another loss in the final game of the year knocked the Colts out of the playoffs.

In finishing with a 7–5 record, the Colts surprised a lot

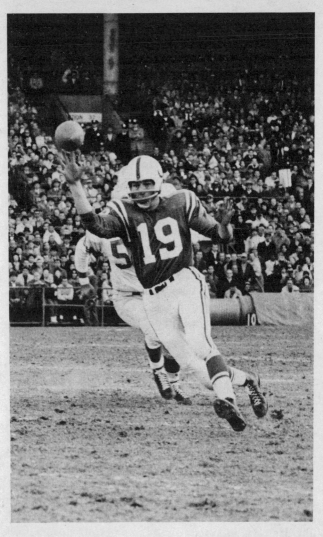

Johnny U. flips a pass to his favorite target, Raymond Berry.

of people. Unitas surprised even more people. Only two years removed from the Pittsburgh sandlots, the 24-year-old quarterback was voted the NFL's Most Valuable Player! Practically out of nowhere, Johnny U. had emerged as the best quarterback in the game. You can bet the Steelers were kicking themselves for never having given Johnny a chance.

After a flying start, Unitas was grounded in the sixth game of the 1958 season. In a 56–0 rout of the Green Bay Packers, Unitas suffered a punctured lung and three cracked ribs. Those were the first in a long line of injuries John would endure in his 19-year career. But nothing could keep him idle for long. John continually amazed coaches and teammates with his desire, competitiveness, and high pain threshold. He may not have been the biggest or strongest of football players, but he certainly was among the toughest.

Three weeks later, after the Packer game, he was back at the helm. Receiving a tremendous ovation from the huge crowd at Baltimore's Memorial Stadium, John immediately dispelled any doubts about his well-being: On his very first play, Unitas fired a 58-yard touchdown pass to the Colts' great halfback, Lenny Moore. Unitas threw another scoring pass later in the contest: The Colts won over the Los Angeles Rams, 34–7.

Baltimore got stronger as the year went on. Leading the Western Conference with an 8–1 mark, the Colts had an opportunity to clinch first place against the San Francisco 49'ers. But after the opening 30 minutes, the Colts looked like anything but a first-place club. The 49'ers had tallied four first-half touchdowns and taken a 27-7 lead. The Colts' only score came on a four-yard run by Unitas. They were getting embarrassed, and Colt Coach Weeb Ewbank didn't like it one bit. He laced into his team at half time.

Stirred up by Ewbank's angry words, the Colts were a different team in the second half. On their first possession, Unitas engineered a 62-yard scoring march to narrow the score to 27–14. The fired-up Colt defense halted the 49'ers, and John went to work again. He faded back and lofted a beautiful pass to Jim Mutscheller for a 50-yard advance. Two plays later, Alan Ameche punched over. Suddenly, the Colts were only down by six. The game had turned around completely.

With Unitas directing the attack brilliantly, there was no stopping Baltimore. John figured the shell-shocked 49'ers expected him to pass, so he crossed them up by handing off to Moore. It couldn't have worked better. Lenny broke a couple of tackles and sprinted away for a 73-yard touchdown. The Colts took the lead for the first time, 28–27.

Unitas concluded the assault with a seven-yard touchdown toss to his favorite receiver, Raymond Berry. It was the twenty-third consecutive game in which Unitas had thrown a touchdown pass, a new NFL record. Before John's astonishing streak ended in 1960, he had thrown scoring passes in 47 straight games. That's a record many NFL experts believe will never be broken.

The stunning comeback against the 49'ers was a great tribute to Unitas, both as a quarterback and as a team leader. "Nobody gave up," commented Ameche, "because John was acting and talking like we were ahead. And pretty soon we were ahead."

The Colts moved into the NFL championship game against the New York Giants in Yankee Stadium. The Colts knew they would have their hands full with the Giants, who had beaten them, 24–21, earlier in the season. But Unitas had been sidelined for that game. Now the Colts were hoping John would make the difference.

Everyone expected an exciting, hard-fought contest. They weren't disappointed. That 1958 championship game is generally considered the greatest football game ever played. In fact, many people credit that heart-stopping contest with catapulting football into the big time among professional sports. It's not hard to see why.

Operating against the league's toughest defense, Unitas ignited the Colts to a 14–3 lead at half time. The big play was a 60-yard bomb to Moore. Unitas's pinpoint passing was giving the New Yorkers fits.

In the third quarter, Unitas and the Colts appeared on the verge of breaking the game open. John led the Colts all the way to the Giants' three-yard line. Knowing the game was on the line, the New York defense stiffened. They stopped Ameche twice and Unitas once. On fourth down, the Colts tried again. But the Giants didn't budge. Ameche was thrown for a loss. The brilliant goal-line stand completely shifted the game's momentum.

The Giants roared back, scoring two touchdowns to take a 17–14 lead. Meanwhile, New York's ferocious pass rush was giving Unitas no time to pass.

The Colts got their last chance when they took over the ball on their own 14-yard line with 1:56 to play.

In his quiet but commanding way, Unitas addressed his teammates: "Okay, now we find out what stuff we're made of." John led by example. If he felt the excruciating pressure, he didn't show it.

After an incompletion, he calmly stepped back and hit Moore for 11 yards. Dropping deep again, he rifled a 25-yard strike to Berry for 25 yards. There was no time for huddles, but that didn't faze Unitas, regarded as perhaps the finest "two-minute" quarterback in NFL history.

He went to Berry again, this time for 16 yards. The Giants were on the run, and Unitas knew it. He faded back and zipped still another pass to Berry for a 21-yard pickup to the New York 13. Seven seconds remained. Steve Myhra came on for a field goal. He made it. The game went into overtime.

It was "sudden death." The first team to score would win. Every play was critical.

The Giants got the ball first, but were unable to mount a drive. The Colts took over at their own 20.

Following a pair of running plays, Unitas dropped to pass on third-and-seven. He hit Ameche cutting across the middle. First down—by inches.

On Unitas's next passing attempt, he was leveled for a 12-yard sack. It was third and 15. Everybody knew he had to pass. Johnny drifted back. The Giants charged. Berry maneuvered into the clear. But Unitas knew his end was short of a first down. The quarterback quickly and calmly waved to Berry to go deeper. He did, and Unitas delivered the pass right on target. It was a 20-yard gain for another first down. The ball was at the Giants' 42. The Colts were on the move.

Having burned the Giants repeatedly through the air, Unitas knew they expected him to stick with the passing game. He moved up to take the snap, and saw that the New York linebackers were prepared to drop back into pass coverage. Unitas quickly changed plays, screaming new signals to his team. John took a few steps back as if to pass, then slipped the ball to Ameche. The Giants were completely fooled. Ameche raced for 23 yards to the 19.

From there, Unitas hit Berry for yards to the New York eight. Everybody expected the Colts to play it safe and go for the easy field goal. But Unitas thought otherwise. He had the Giants where he wanted them. Probably no other quarterback in the game would have had the courage to call for a pass in that situation. But John Unitas did—and he completed it for 8 yards to Mutscheller. Again, his brilliant play-calling had caught the Giants by surprise.

Two plays later, 8 minutes and 15 seconds into overtime, Ameche plunged over to give the Colts their first NFL championship. It was no surprise when Unitas was named the game's Most Valuable Player. Against the best defense in the NFL, John had completed 26 of 40 passes for a playoff-record 349 yards. It was one of the greatest performances in NFL history.

John repeated the trick in 1959, when he led all NFL passers in every important category and guided his team into the championship once more. The opponent? The New York Giants. But this time, Unitas needed no last-second heroics to pull it out. The Colts thoroughly dominated the game, winning 31–16 for their second straight NFL crown. Unitas was again selected as Most Valuable Player of the title game. It was another routine day for Johnny U.—18 completions in 29 attempts for 264 yards and 2 touchdowns.

Although the Colts didn't win another championship until 1970, they continued to be one of the best teams in the NFL. In fact, they amassed the best won-lost record in football in the 1960s. There was no argument about the biggest reason for their success. It was Number 19, Johnny U.

Named the NFL's player of the decade in the sixties and the greatest quarterback in the NFL's first 50 years, Unitas continued to pile up records and awards. But he would have gladly traded any of them for more championships. "Records are nice, I guess," said the reserved, humble quarterback, "but they don't mean that much to me. I just like to play football and win games."

Simple and honest, that's the essence of John Unitas. Even toward the end of his brilliant career, he never

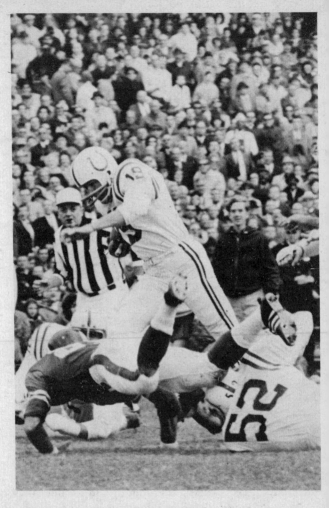

Keepin' 'em honest—Johnny on the run

seemed completely comfortable in the spotlight. He was forever praising his teammates and downplaying his own personal accomplishments.

And what accomplishments they were! By the time he retired in 1974 at the age of 41, John had virtually rewritten the record books. A three-time NFL Most Valuable Player, he established new marks for passing yardage (40,239); touchdown passes (290); passes attempted (5,186); passes completed (2,830); most consecutive games throwing a touchdown pass (47); most games, 300 or more yards passing (26); and most seasons leading league in touchdown passes (4). Fran Tarkenton of the Minnesota Vikings has since eclipsed a number of these records. But that by no means diminishes the greatness of Unitas.

On the field and off, John always seemed to take everything in stride. He rarely lost his cool. Nothing seemed to ruffle him—not even retirement.

"I came into the league without any fuss," he said quietly after 18 record-breaking years in the NFL, "and I'd just as soon leave it that way. There's no difference that I can see in retiring from pro football or quitting a job at the Pennsylvania Railroad. I did something I wanted to do, and went as far as I could go."

As far as anyone could go.

GEORGE BLANDA

If George Blanda could have bottled and sold his secret, he would have become an instant millionaire. Because George Blanda did what people all over the world—athletes and nonathletes alike—dream about. George Blanda defied the march of time.

For, at 48 years old, Blanda was still playing professional football. That's nearly two decades past the time when most players call it quits. In a game in which the average career spans about six years, "Old George," as the gray-haired star liked to call himself, played for more than a quarter of a century—26 years to be exact.

His durability is never likely to be equaled. Quarterback Earl Morrall (twenty-one seasons) and defensive end Jim Marshall (starting his twentieth in 1979) are the only other players in the history of the game to last more than 20 years.

Blanda was a rookie with the Chicago Bears in 1949. By the time he retired in 1976—340 games later—most of the men he was playing with had not even been born in 1949.

Once, during his fourth decade in pro football, the ageless Blanda prompted one fan to joke, "Why, this George Blanda is as good as his father, who used to play for the Houston Oilers!" It was, of course, the same George Blanda.

A fine quarterback and a deadly accurate place-kicker, Blanda holds the NFL career mark for most points scored—2,002. Most experts agree that this record will be practically impossible to break. After all, when will there be another football player who lasts 26 years? Probably never. The closest player to Blanda is Fred Cox, who scored almost 600 fewer points in his long career with the Minnesota Vikings.

George's incredible scoring total includes 9 touchdowns, 335 field goals (a record), and 943 extra points (also a record). He attempted 959 extra points in his career, which means he missed only 16 conversions in 26 years! In one stretch, George connected on 156 consecutive extra-point attempts.

The name Blanda is also sprinkled throughout the NFL passing records. As the Houston Oilers' quarterback in 1964, he set records for most passes attempted (68) and most passes completed (37) in the same game. Earlier in his Oiler career, Blanda established a new mark for most touchdown passes in a season (36) and tied the record for most touchdown passes in a game (7).

On the negative side of the ledger, Blanda has the dubious distinction of possessing the record for most interceptions in a season (42 in 1962). It should be added that George was under constant defensive pressure that season. "Our linemen were confused about calling their blocking assignments, and the other teams caught on in a hurry and red-dogged the heck out of George," one teammate recalled.

When you play the game as long as George did, you're bound to have a lot of ups and downs. And George had a

"Old George" fires one of his record-breaking 37 completions against the Buffalo Bills.

healthy portion of both. Ironically, most of his "downs" came in his earlier years, when he was in his physical prime. But he endured the tough times and went on to have some of his greatest moments after he turned 40.

Blanda's first professional seasons were not all that eventful. A star quarterback and kicker at the University of Kentucky, Blanda was made a reserve linebacker and defensive back by the Bears. He wasn't particularly happy with his situation.

Following his rookie year in 1949, he was traded to the Baltimore Colts. He enjoyed a good season of kicking with the Colts, but that didn't stop the club from trading him to the Green Bay Packers. Young Blanda barely had a chance with the Packers, who released him before the 1951 season. The much-traveled youngster then came back to the Bears. Coach George Halas decided he might be able to use Blanda after all.

It was a wise decision. Blanda blossomed into a fine quarterback and one of the top kickers in the league. He remained with the Bears until he retired for a season in 1959. Relegated to the backup quarterback slot for the previous several seasons and disenchanted with his earnings, Blanda chose to go into business. But he wasn't away from football for long.

The American Football League was formed in 1960, and its founders knew that name players were essential to help the league get off the ground. George Blanda was a name player. A couple of teams expressed interest in the 32-year-old Blanda, including Coach Sid Gillman of the Los Angeles Chargers (the club moved to San Diego the following year). But Blanda signed with the Houston Oilers.

Led by Blanda's 27 touchdown passes and 2,694 yards passing, the explosive Oilers made it into the AFL's first championship game in 1960. The opponent was the Los Angeles Chargers. Old George fired three touchdown passes, including an 88-yarder to Billy Cannon, and added a field goal to spark Houston to a 24–16 victory.

George was even better in 1961, when he was named the AFL's Player of the Year and again guided the Oilers to a championship. While connecting on 187 of his 362 passes, Blanda established his record of 36 touchdown passes and threw for 3,330 yards.

The Oilers made it to the championship game once more in 1962, but after that the franchise went into a prolonged slide. The team was in chaos; it had five coaches in five years. Blanda continued to fill the air, throwing for more than 3,000 yards in 1963 and 1964. But the team was no longer winning. And Old George became the target of a lot of boos.

"All that booing is a natural reaction," George remarked. "When you lose, the quarterback gets it. It's an occupational hazard. The world loves a winner. You can't win all the time."

After the worst season in the club's brief history in 1966, the Oilers decided to go with a youth movement. The 39-year-old George Blanda, thought to be too old to play football any longer, was handed his walking papers. He didn't walk for long. The Oakland Raiders promptly signed him. Thus began the last—and most glamorous—era of George Blanda's phenomenal career.

Working relentlessly to keep his 40-year-old body in prime shape, the man too old to play went on to have himself quite a year in 1967. George led the AFL in scoring with 116 points. In two games against his old teammates, Blanda booted a total of eight field goals, accounting for more points than the entire Houston team.

Playing behind first-stringer Daryle Lamonica, George didn't see much action at quarterback anymore. But when he *was* pressed into duty, he showed that the old magic was still there.

Lamonica was injured prior to a 1968 game against the Denver Broncos, and George stepped in to throw four touchdown passes, including a 94-yarder to Warren Wells. That's the longest touchdown in Raider history.

With the Raiders romping, 40–7, late in the game, Blanda trotted off the field and pointed to the Raiders' Number 3 quarterback, 36-year-old Cotton Davidson. "Okay, you can put the kid in now," cracked Blanda to Coach John Rauch.

Afterward, Denver Coach Lou Saban, infuriated that a 41-year-old quarterback could pick apart his team, snapped, "That old man ought to retire and get out of our hair!" Retirement was the furthest thing from Old George's mind.

Following another solid season of kicking in 1969, Blanda received a severe jolt to his pride early in the 1970 preseason: The Raiders had put him on waivers. Not a single team in the NFL claimed him.

Angry and hurt, George contemplated quitting—until Raider General Manager Al Davis talked to him. Davis explained that he had put Blanda on waivers only because he wanted to protect some of the younger players. The general manager reassured his ageless kicker that he was still a vital part of the team. "If anybody had picked you up," Davis told Blanda, "we'd have yanked you right off the waiver list."

George started slowly that season. He missed his only field goal attempt in a season-opening loss to Cincinnati. Then, a week later against San Diego, Blanda came on for a 32-yard field goal try with the score tied at 27 and under a minute to play. George had made two field goals already, but a stiff crosswind carried this one wide. The newspapers seemed ready to pack George's bags for him. One reporter wrote, "Blanda the kicker is probably fading away. He appears unsteady at field-goal time..."

But Blanda had been through adversity before. And the old warhorse wasn't about to hang them up yet....not by a long shot. With his critics looking on in stunned silence, Blanda went on to probably the greatest sequence of dramatic, game-winning heroics in NFL history.

In the sixth game of the season, Lamonica suffered an injury in the first quarter against the Pittsburgh Steelers. Raider Coach John Madden called on Blanda in favor of Kenny Stabler, who was an untested youngster at the time.

Blanda responded by firing 3 touchdown passes, completing 7 of his 12 aerials, and kicking a 27-yard field goal and 4 extra points to lead Oakland to a 31–14 victory. He was awarded the game ball by his teammates.

Lamonica returned the next week, but the Raiders were trailing the Kansas City Chiefs by three points with less than a minute to play.

With the ball on their own 20, the Raiders had one last chance to avert defeat. Quickly, Lamonica drilled four completions to move the Raiders to the Chiefs' 41 with just eight seconds to play. It was time for George Blanda. Some 60,000 screaming, arm-flailing Kansas City fans did their best to distract Old George. To no avail. Blanda boomed the game-tying 3-pointer from 48 yards out!

"I knew it was good as soon as I hit," said George, matter-of-factly.

Two weeks in a row, Blanda's clutch passing and kicking had given the Raiders a victory and a tie. There was more to come—much more.

The next week, against the Cleveland Browns, Lamonica was sidelined with a shoulder injury in the final quarter. The Raiders trailed, 20–13. Enter Blanda. Old Steel Nerves calmly marched the Raiders 55 yards downfield before drilling a 14-yard scoring pass to Warren Wells. George's extra point knotted the score at 20.

Desperately trying to pull out the victory, Cleveland quarterback Bill Nelsen came out passing. But Oakland intercepted a pass, and with just over 30 seconds to play, Blanda came on again. With an eye on the clock, he carefully led the Raiders to the Cleveland 45. Three seconds remained.

Blanda lined up for a 52-yard field goal, an almost impossible distance, even without the heart-stopping pressure. He waited for the snap, stepped into the ball, and slammed it through the uprights. The Raiders mobbed him. He had done it again—this time with his longest field goal as a Raider.

A horde of reporters greeted Blanda in the locker room. "Was this your greatest thrill in football?" one asked.

"I never say, 'This is my biggest thrill.' It's what you can do tomorrow that's important," replied the 21-year veteran.

George hadn't run out of miracles yet. Seven days later, with the Raiders trailing the Broncos, 19–17, with four minutes to play, Blanda replaced Lamonica. All Blanda did was engineer an 80-yard touchdown drive, the final 20 coming on a scoring strike to Fred Biletnikoff. The Raiders won again, 24–19.

"This is getting so routine, his performance probably won't even make the wires," joked Coach Madden.

George Blanda, age 43, was suddenly the biggest name in pro football. He was written about in all the newspapers from coast to coast. "I can see these last-second heroics happening for a week or maybe two," said one writer, "but four! ... Come on, I just won't believe any more of this. This is supposed to be the NFL—not a fairy tale."

The fairy tale wasn't over yet. The Chargers and the Raiders played to a 17–17 tie the following week—for 59 minutes and 53 seconds. Then, with 7 seconds to go, the magic man did it again, connecting on a game-winning field goal from 16 yards out.

Never before in pro-football history had there been such an incredible string of one-man miracle finishes, each in the face of almost unbearable pressure. Old George single-handedly carried the Raiders to a divisional title. So much for Blanda fading away....

That unprecedented, storybook 1970 season was the crowning achievement of George Blanda's astonishing career in pro football. Indeed, how could it *not* have been? He gave the Raiders five more valuable years of service after that, retiring in 1976, just a few weeks shy of his 49th birthday.

The obvious question that arises about this ageless wonder is: How did he do it? How did he manage to play—and excel—at a young man's game when he was into his forties?

Those who know Blanda, point to his fierce determination and competitiveness. "The thing that always impressed me about George," observed one member of the Raiders, "is his competitiveness in everything he does. Whether it's a football game, a round of golf, a card game on the team plane, he is an intensely competitive person. He plays hard and he wants to win."

Wally Lemm, a former coach of George's with the Oilers, agreed. "He's the greatest competitor I've ever been around," declared Lemm.

The Ageless Wonder shows little emotion after scoring his 2,000th point in 1975.

A proud, confident, almost defiant man, George Blanda pushed and pummeled himself without end to remain in superb physical condition. Driven by critics who predicted he was washed up as far back as the early 1960s, Blanda seemed to grow more determined by the year.

He was as determined as ever to play football in 1976. But the Raiders seemed equally determined to give his job to 22-year-old rookie Fred Steinfort.

George Blanda was put on waivers, and this time he wasn't reclaimed. Twenty-six years after his rookie season, age finally caught up with George Blanda.

Maybe he didn't defy the march of time after all. But one thing is certain: This surefire Hall-of-Famer came a lot closer to doing it than any other football player ever will.

MERLIN OLSEN

Somehow, Merlin Olsen never fit the image most people have of a lineman in the National Football League. You know the linemen—those massive, brutish beasts who man the trenches every week, beating each other to a pulp.

Merlin Olsen *looked* the part, all right, at 6-foot-5 and 275 pounds. And in his 15 brilliant seasons as defensive tackle with the Los Angeles Rams, he *played* the part to perfection. But Merlin's likeness to that popular image of linemen ended right there.

An articulate, intelligent man (he was a Phi Beta Kappa and second in his class at Utah State), Merlin bristles whenever he hears line play referred to as "the Pit" and linemen called everything from goons to gorillas. That notion is wrong, and Merlin has gone out of his way to try to change it. Of the "animal" reputation that linemen are often saddled with Olsen says, "It's so much against my nature and the way I feel about the game . . . I don't feel that way when I'm playing or toward the guys against whom I'm playing. I have a great deal of respect for most of the guys I play against. Some of the best friends I have are the guards I play opposite. We may be knocking the heck out of each other, but there's a certain aura of professionalism. We walk off with our arms around each other. That's the kind of game I want to play. I don't want to play a game where I become an animal.

"Violence is built into pro football, all right," the Ram great continued, "but the game is played above the violence. It's controlled. If I wanted to, I could go after quarterbacks at the knees and knock out a couple every year. But I don't. I'll give them a helmet or a forearm in the chest. I want to test them. But I don't want to cripple them.

"The old image of the stupid defensive lineman is dead," asserted Merlin. "Our game has become very sophisticated."

Merlin related a story that illustrates how football can be played "above the violence." It was a game against the New York Giants.

"We intercepted a pass and I was going full speed downfield," Merlin recalled. "The first guy to come into my sights was Tucker Frederickson, the Giants' fullback. He sees me when I'm two steps away from him, and he knows he's dead. So he raises his hand as if to surrender. And I stopped. I don't know why, except that Tucker made communication with me to the effect that he would not tackle the guy who made the interception if I wouldn't hit him. It was very strange."

Not every player would have stopped as Olsen did; some guys would have flattened Frederickson without a thought. But that wasn't Merlin Olsen's style. He played as hard as anyone in the league, but he always drew the line between controlled violence and wanton violence.

Olsen's illustrious career with the Rams began in 1962, after he was voted a two-time All-American at Utah State. A highly touted first-round draft choice, Merlin remembered, "I signed for a $15,000 bonus and two

$20,000 contracts—the best deal ever made for a rookie lineman up to that time."

The Ram coaches had no questions about the massive rookie's ability, but they did have a question about where to put him. Merlin was a defensive tackle in college, and the Rams' defensive coaches wanted to keep him there. But the offensive coaches, thinking Merlin would make a great guard, wanted him for their unit.

The Rams experimented with Merlin at guard during one scrimmage. The experiment did not last long.

"On my first play, I was supposed to pull and trap Deacon Jones [the Rams' great defensive end]," Olsen related. "But just as I came out of my stance, Deacon came across and almost took my head off. I couldn't even breathe for awhile. I found out later that someone was giving Deacon the snap count. Anyway, I soon moved to defense and stayed there forever after."

Once on defense, Olsen wasted no time in establishing himself as one of the premier tackles in the league. He was named to the Pro Bowl his first season—and every year after until 1976. His 14 consecutive Pro Bowl appearances is an NFL record.

Playing alongside Deacon Jones, Olsen was part of perhaps the best and most-feared left-side tandem in football history. Indeed, in the late 1960s, the entire Ram defensive line—Olsen, Jones, Rosey Grier, and Lamar Lundy—became known as the Fearsome Foursome.

That was just the first of an awesome series of offensive-wrecking lines that Merlin anchored in his 15 years with the Rams. Later, his comrades included Roger Brown, Diron Talbert, and Coy Bacon. After that, it was Fred Dryer, Jack Youngblood, and Larry Brooks. And always, there was Number 74—Merlin Olsen—the rock-hard stalwart at defensive tackle.

Olsen (74) fights off a blocker.

Year in and year out, Olsen gave fits to the men who lined up opposite him. Gene Hickerson, an all-pro himself as a guard for the Cleveland Browns, once said of Olsen, "There's no way I can handle that guy. No way."

"I don't think I've ever seen a defensive lineman play any better football," added Tommy Prothro, a former Ram coach.

Strength, quickness, and a thorough knowledge of his position—those were the key ingredients to Merlin's enduring success. "I think it takes as many years to develop a top-flight defensive lineman as it does a quarterback," Merlin remarked. "Intelligence, determination, concentration, deception, agility, and quickness are all my weapons as much as are my size and toughness.

"But," he added, "without size and toughness, none of the rest would be of any use."

Merlin went on to describe his approach to his job. "My pass rush is more or less instinctive," he said. "I don't look for the ball. I feel the ball. You feel as much as you see.

"I'm pretty strong," Olsen continued, "but I can seldom run over a good blocker. What I'm trying to do is make him move himself. If he doesn't move, he's usually got me. First, I try to beat him hard inside. He can't stay put against that. On the next play, I might start inside, then stop, throw him, and slip outside. It's a game of movement."

And Olsen's movement, more often than not, resulted in an ineffective run, an incomplete pass—or a quarterback on his backside. He would disrupt the offense any way he could.

Having spent most of his career frustrating would-be blockers and creating havoc in offensive backfields,

Merlin was a frequent victim of offensive holding. "The better you are," he observed, "the more they're driven by desperation to illegal tactics. I've had men hold me on the opening play of the game, before they've even tried to stop me fairly. I hate it, but it's difficult to detect and you just have to live with it."

Not only was Olsen one of the best defensive linemen in NFL history, he also was one of the most durable. From his rookie year to the day he retired in 1976, Merlin started in 210 consecutive games, a club record. That's a remarkable feat for any player; but it's practically unheard of for a defensive lineman.

Twice honored as the Rams' Most Valuable Player—another rarity for a defensive lineman—Merlin was voted to the All-NFL team five years in a row (1966-70) and to the Pro Bowl, 15 times. He also was named Player of the Year by the Maxwell Club.

There have been few linemen who have been so consistently outstanding for so long as Merlin Olsen. Merlin sees that as the crowning achievement of his superb career. "If you ask me what I'm most proud of," he said, "it would have to be my consistency. I think that's the test of a real champion. There are a lot of people who can do it for one or two games or even over a single season, but staying in there when you're losing or when you don't feel like being there, that's when you find out what's down inside you."

Merlin was a real champion, even if the Rams, despite being among the best teams in the game for most of his career, could never make the same claim. There were a lot of near misses for the Rams; the one Merlin remembers most was the heartbreaking 23–20 loss to the Minnesota Vikings in the 1969 Western Conference championship game.

Merlin and Isiah Robertson (58) help contain an elusive man—O. J. Simpson.

"I remember walking across the parking lot in Bloomington after the game," said Merlin. "I didn't have a jacket because I loaned it to someone, and he didn't return it. It was bitter cold with an icy wind, and I didn't even feel it. I was already numb. I was really low—dangerously low.

"I learned something from that," Merlin added. "Other events in your life are much more important than a game. I don't plunge that deep anymore. I won't allow it."

Another of Olsen's most memorable moments was just a little bit happier. In the final minutes of his last game before the hometown fans in the Los Angeles Memorial Coliseum, over 50,000 fans chanted, "We want Olsen... We want Olsen..."

Coach Chuck Knox then sent the Ram great onto the field for one last play. The massive crowd responded with a thunderous standing ovation.

"I've never seen these fans do that for any other player," said one astounded observer.

"This was a special day for me," said Merlin emotionally, "and not just because the cheering gave me a lump in my throat big enough to keep me from talking for a week. It was special also because of the way we played. Everything we did was right." The Rams had routed the Atlanta Falcons that day, 59–0.

Merlin was always one player who kept the game in perspective. "You have to have priorities in life," Merlin stated. "A job should be important, but when it's more important than anything in the world, you're in trouble."

Merlin Olsen is a sensitive, thoughtful, and talented man. "I never felt football was the only thing I could do," said Merlin. "It was the thing I decided to do."

A couple of more Merlin Olsens, and the image of linemen just might change.

JOE NAMATH

Super Bowl III was just a couple of days away. Joe Namath, the young, brassy, rocket-armed quarterback of the New York Jets, was relaxing at poolside of a Miami Hotel.

Quickly, he found himself surrounded by a host of news-hungry reporters. They were looking for a good story, a fresh angle to drum up interest in a game that most people thought would be nothing but a Super Mismatch.

After all, the NFL-champion Baltimore Colts, regarded as one of the finest teams of all time, had been installed as three-touchdown favorites over the Jets. And many experts felt that this was being kind to the Jets, that the Colts would likely win by 30 or 40 points. With a high-powered offense and the NFL's best defense, the Colts had cruised to a 13–1 record during the regular season. That was the best mark by an NFL club since 1942, when the Chicago Bears were 11–0.

In the two previous Super Bowls, the AFL teams had been badly outclassed. And the overwhelming consensus was that this year's AFL representative, the Jets, stood even less of a chance to win. "The Jets," cracked one reporter, "should seriously consider not showing up."

So you can imagine the shock that went through the

press corps when Namath stated flatly, "We'll win. I guarantee it." One disbelieving journalist asked the quarterback to repeat himself. Joe gladly obliged.

The reporters could scarcely believe their ears. It was the brashest, boldest, and seemingly the most absurd prediction ever made.

But Broadway Joe Namath backed it up. The flamboyant quarterback directed the Jets to a 16-7 triumph in one of the greatest upsets in football history. Voted the game's Most Valuable Player, Namath befuddled the Colts with his superb play-calling and pinpoint passing. He completed 17 of 29 passes for 206 yards.

Lots of people scoffed at Namath's outrageous guarantee, but nobody could scoff at his performance. "Namath did everything," said Colt Coach Don Shula dejectedly. "He knows what's happening and mixes his plays very well. His quickness took away our blitz. He beat our blitz more than we beat him."

"Namath was fabulous," raved Jet Coach Weeb Ewbank. "He didn't make a bad call."

Just after the final gun sounded, the man who had put himself on the line trotted jubilantly off the field, waving one finger over his head. Yes sir, Joe, you called the shot: The Jets were indeed number one.

"This has to be the most satisfying win in my life," Namath said in the steamy, riotous Jet locker room. Never at a loss for words, Namath then had a brief message for all the reporters around the country who had dismissed his prediction as utterly ridiculous. "I hope they eat their pencils and pads," declared Joe.

Perhaps more than any other athlete in recent times, Joe Namath has always had a way of being in the spotlight. Long before he fired his first professional pass,

Namath guaranteed it—and Namath did it: Super
Joe fires against the Colts in Super Bowl III.

he was a widely celebrated signal-caller. Then he zoomed into prominence the moment he signed on the Jets' dotted line for a reported $400,000.

With rugged good looks, a shotgun for an arm, and charisma to spare, the former University of Alabama All-American became an instant and unrivaled gate attraction. He was exactly what the AFL needed.

Only five years old when Namath arrived on the scene in 1965, The AFL was a struggling, under-publicized league, desperately trying to gain equal status with the older NFL. The AFL had many fine players, but it lacked the glamor and stature of the NFL. Joe Namath, more than any other player, helped to change all that.

It wasn't just that he had the talent to lead the AFL to its first Super Bowl championship. His impact went far beyond that. He was a name, a big name—probably the biggest in pro football—and he belonged to the Jets and the AFL. He gave the league stature and, even more importantly, publicity.

Everything Namth did was hot news—partly because he was playing in New York, the media capital of the country, but mostly because he was Joe Namath. He was the first long-hair in professional sports, his wavy brown locks flowing from the bottom of his helmet. That was hot news. He lived in a posh New York apartment, equipped with a round bed and white llama rug. That was hot news. He was a man-about-town in New York, frequenting the fashionable nightspots. That, too, was hot news.

In an era when facial hair was taboo for athletes, he sported a Fu Manchu mustache. Then a manufacturer of shaving products paid him a reported $10,000 to shave it off. That was hot news. He wore white shoes on the football field, and even that was hot news.

Joe's flair for publicity concerned some officials in the AFL, notably Milt Woodard, the league president. Woodard once asked Namath to "conform with the generally accepted idea of an American athlete's appearance." But Namath was his own man. He was someone special, someone different. And it was a good thing for the AFL. Whether he got good publicity or bad, Joe Willie Namath somehow always managed to keep himself—and his league—in the headlines.

James Reston, well-known columnist for the *New York Times*, once wrote, "Joe Namath is one of the most interesting symbols of the young.... He defies both the people who hate playboys and the people who hate bully boys. He is something special: A long-haired hardhat, the anti-hero of the sports world."

Even without Namath, the AFL almost certainly would have achieved its goal of equality with the NFL. But, without Joe, it wouldn't have happened as quickly as it did.

As flamboyant as Joe was off the field, he was just as flamboyant on it. Gifted with one of the strongest arms of any passer in NFL history, Namath was a daring, gambling quarterback right from his rookie year in 1965. He began his career impressively, completing 164 passes in 340 attempts for 2,220 yards and 15 touchdowns. He was voted the AFL's Rookie of the Year.

Namath was at the top of the heap in the pass-happy AFL in 1966. He threw more times (471, an average of nearly 34 passes a game) for more completions (232) and more yards (3,379) than any other passer in the league. A young and improving team, the Jets finished with a 6–6–2 record. But with a shaky defense, among other weaknesses, they were still a couple of years away from the Super Bowl.

In just two years, the gimpy-kneed quarterback from Beaver Falls, Pennsylvania, had already established himself as one of the premier passers in the game. Said one AFL coach: "There are two factors in judging a quarterback—preparing for him and playing him. Joe Namath scares you both times. When you play the Jets, your whole approach to the game involves him. You're conscious of him, it disrupts your plans. In the game, no matter what the down or distance, he's capable of hitting a big play on you."

Spectacular! That's the only way to describe Joe's 1967 season. He set a new record with an amazing 4,007 yards passing. No quarterback had ever broken the 4,000 mark in a season. Namath's explosive right arm also accounted for 26 touchdowns, as he again led the league in attempts (491) and completions (258). Improving to 8–5–1, the Jets narrowly missed qualifying for the playoffs.

Maturing into a fine play-caller and reader of defenses, Namath also seemed to develop into a smarter, more selective passer in 1968. He still loved to throw the bomb and to riddle defenses with his deep, pinpoint passing. But he put the ball up over a hundred times less than he did in 1967. He controlled the ball more, manipulated defenses more, though he never let his opponents forget that he could strike for the big one at any time with stunning and game-breaking suddenness.

The Jets, meanwhile, had grown into a first-class team. They finished atop the AFL's Eastern Division with an 11–3 record. Led by the league's Most Valuable Player—Joe Namath—the Jets squared off against the defending-champion Oakland Raiders in the title match.

Late in the game, Oakland scored to take a 23–20 lead. The Jets took over at their own 32. The game was on the line. And Broadway Joe went to work.

With his lightning-fast release, Namath drilled a 10-yard pass to a split end, George Sauer. Then, dropping deep into the pocket, Joe cut loose the bomb of bombs—a pass that traveled some 70 yards in the air. Nerveless Namath laid it right in flanker Don Maynard's arms at the six-yard line. Two passes . . . and the Raiders were on the ropes.

From the six, Namath faded back once more. His receivers were covered. Namath patiently waited until the last possible moment. He spotted Maynard, who was closely covered deep in the end zone. Joe fired. Touchdown!

"I heard the ball hum," said running back Matt Snell later. "I heard that ball go by me." That hummer won the AFL championship for the New York Jets. Namath had engineered the winning drive in only 55 seconds.

Two weeks later came Namath's ultimate triumph—the Super Bowl victory over the Colts.

In 1969, Joe once again led the Jets to the AFL championship game. But the New Yorkers could not repeat, losing to the Kansas City Chiefs, who went on to stun the Minnesota Vikings and capture the AFL's second straight Super Bowl.

The next couple of seasons were, on the whole, not the happiest of times for Namath. In the fifth game of the 1970 campaign, he was blistering the Colts with 34 completions in 62 attempts. Then disaster struck. Colt tackle Billy Ray Smith charged through the line and crashed into Joe. The quarterback suffered a broken wrist. He was finished for the year. So were the Jets.

Although plagued by the most fragile knees in the business, Namath had not, until then, missed a game in his Jets career. He came back raring to go in 1971. He was the same old Namath in an exhibition game against the

Jet fans winced when their fragile-kneed hero took
lumps like this one from Baltimore's Stan White.

Detroit Lions, passing and running the offense beautifully.

Suddenly, the Jets fumbled. The Lions' middle linebacker, Mike Lucci, recovered and started upfield. Namath gave chase and was knocked down by a Lion blocker. He shrieked in agony and clutched his leg, writhing in pain. It had happened again. He was idled for 10 games.

Namath's debut that year was truly heroic. Bob Davis, the man who had replaced Namath, suffered an ankle injury in the second quarter against the San Francisco 49'ers. Joe got the call. The Jet fans gave their returning hero a stadium-rocking ovation. Joe responded with three touchdown passes—after over a year of inactivity— to bring the Jets to within three points. His last-second pass was picked off in the end zone, but the fans still cheered Namath as the game ended. As well they should have. He had thrown for 258 yards on 11-for-28 passing and had come within a whisker of pulling the game out.

Joe Willie could still zing that pigskin with the best of them. In fact, creaky knees, complete lack of mobility, and all, Namath was voted the most coveted quarterback in a 1971 poll of NFL coaches.

With a healthy Namath at the helm, the Jets got off to a flying start in 1972. Joe put 41 points on the board against Buffalo in the opener. The next stop was in Baltimore against the Colts. It was one of the most memorable games in football history, a spectacular old-fashioned shootout between two of the best ball-slingers ever to step on the field, Joe Namath and Johnny Unitas. That the Jets won, 44-34, almost seemed incidental compared with the performances of these two great quarterbacks.

It was the last hurrah in the brilliant career of the aging master, Johnny U. And what a last hurrah it was! In completing a career-high 26 passes, Unitas fired for 376 yards. What's even more incredible is that he was upstaged by Joe Namath.

Broadway Joe had the third best passing day in NFL history, ransacking the Colt secondary for 496 yards! And he did it on only 15 completions (in 28 attempts), for an average gain of 33 yards a shot. He rifled six touchdown passes, four of them for 65 yards or more. Three of the scoring strikes came within 89 seconds of each other. It was probably the greatest long-range-passing exhibition of all time. And it was accomplished against a deep zone defense designed to take away Namath's long passing game. Undaunted, Namath repeatedly sent his receivers deep, and drilled pass after pass right into the heart of the zone. Only a quarterback with a supreme arm—and supreme self-confidence—could have done it.

Joe Namath has never been short on self-confidence. "I'm convinced I'm better than anybody else," said Joe, always one to speak his mind. "I've been convinced of that for quite awhile. I haven't seen anything out there that I couldn't do and do well. Out there playing, I get annoyed at myself for doing something wrong. Sometimes I tell myself, 'You're not too good,' and that helps me play better because then I tell myself, 'You're the best, darn it, do it right.'"

To be sure, forthright statements like that have brought Namath a good share of criticism. His critics point out that, for much of Joe's career, the Jets were barely a .500 team. "And isn't winning games the ultimate measure of a quarterback?" they ask. Others talk about his interception rate, which was high, particularly early in his career. He has also been criticized for his completion percentage, which was about 50 percent.

Joe has addressed these points a number of times. As

for his completion percentage, he said, "I could have completed 80 percent, if I dropped the ball off to my backs like they do in their [NFL] league."

Indeed, Namath rarely threw the short, safe pass. A fearless game-breaking passer, he loved the aggressive air attack, passing in times and places others wouldn't dare. That wide-open philosophy led inevitably to some interceptions, and they sometimes hurt the Jets. But they never came close to overshadowing his positive contributions.

As for the Jets' record, many experts believe that, with the exception of a couple of years, the team was simply not much better than average. Don Maynard, Namath's favorite passing target, once said, "Joe is so great that he makes up for any weaknesses we have in other spots."

Writer Larry Merchant remarked of Namath once: "He is Napoleon without an army, and every week he has to take Moscow. Still, reports of his death are greatly exaggerated."

Namath judged himself and the performance of the Jets this way: "There are guys that can do things better than I can, mainly running the football and being more mobile. But I don't know for a fact if anyone reads defenses better than I do. I don't know what goes through their minds. I don't see their films every game. But I do my job well. I don't get fooled very often. And a great percentage of the time I'm right in what I'm doing out there."

He continued, "I don't care who you are or what team you're with. You have to have a team to excel."

Although Namath led the league in 1972 with 2,816 yards and tied for tops with 19 touchdowns, the Jets, after their impressive start, slumped to 7–7. Joe was finally healthy again, but the Super Bowl team had become old.

The Jets continued to struggle over the next several

seasons, despite some outstanding play from their signal-caller. Idled for most of 1973 with a shoulder separation, Joe came back in 1974 to pitch for 2,616 yards and 20 touchdowns.

By the end of the Jets' disastrous 3–11 season in 1976, it was obvious the club had to be completely rebuilt. "And I'm too old to be in a rebuilding program," said the 33-year-old Namath with typical candor.

With his own blessing, Joe was released by the Jets. Broadway Joe, the glamorous darling of the New York sports scene for more than a decade, headed west.

In the land of sunshine, Joe hoped to culminate his brilliant career with another Super Bowl championship, this time as a Los Angeles Ram. This time, though, the dream did not pan out. After signing for a reported $450,000, Joe started only the first few games before being lifted in favor of the younger, more mobile Pat Haden. The Rams did not make it to the Super Bowl.

But Joe Namath couldn't have been too unhappy, as he announced his retirement in 1978. He had had many days in the sun during his heralded 13-year tenure as a professional quarterback.

And the brightest day of all had come, ironically, on a cloudy Sunday in Miami, January 12, 1969: Super Bowl III. This was the day Namath was given a new name: Super Joe.

"No matter what else this marvelous quarterback called Joe Namath does," observed writer Eric S. Menges, "he has secured his place in football history. He led his league out of the shadows. Only Joe Namath could have done that. He guaranteed a Super Bowl victory in the face of the most overwhelming of odds. Only Joe Namath could have done that. Then, with an impeccable performance, he delivered. And only Joe Namath could have done that."

FRAN TARKENTON

A Scrambler. The label haunted Fran Tarkenton from the moment he dodged his first lumbering lineman as an NFL rookie in 1961.

Francis Asbury Tarkenton didn't fit the popular conception of what an NFL quarterback should be. At 6-feet and 180 pounds, he was deemed too small and not strong enough. He did not have a cannon for an arm. And most objectionable of all, he was not a standard drop-back passer.

Oh, sometimes he would stay in the pocket, if he got adequate protection. But if a burly, 275-pound defensive tackle was about to break him in two, Francis's keen survival instinct told him to avoid such encounters—by scrambling.

And that was heresy to a lot of NFL followers. People often are resistant to change, and that's what Tarkenton's style represented. Very rarely did you see the big-name quarterbacks of that era—Y. A. Tittle, John Unitas, and Sonny Jurgensen, among others—darting around the backfield.

But none of them, however great they were, possessed Tarkenton's unique abilities. Quick, nimble-footed, and amazingly elusive, Francis brought some new weapons to the position—scrambling and rushing. His style received a great deal of criticism from many members of the NFL's old guard.

Gino Marchetti, the Baltimore Colts' outstanding defensive end, summarized the attitude toward Tarkenton's innovations. Speaking after a frustrating—and futile—afternoon of trying to track Tarkenton down, Marchetti commented, "Personally, I'm not a man to bear grudges. But there are defensive ends in this league who don't think they should be playing foxes and hounds.... The reason is that lots of them are fat and out of shape, and something terrible could happen to Francis if they get mad some day... it's the kid I'm thinking about."

Then the Colt great added, "The kid will never last more than two or three years."

Gino was only off by about 15 years. Francis didn't call it quits until after the 1978 season. His record-shattering career spanned 18 years. And he needed most of those years to convince people that he was truly a great quarterback.

"It took a long time," observed Tarkenton, "for established pro-football writers and pro-football people to accept me because I wasn't in the classic mold of what they thought a quarterback should be. I wasn't big enough, I wasn't strong enough, and, of all things, I actually ran out of the pocket. That was a dastardly thing to do—for a quarterback to scramble around. Of course, they said I'd get killed. They said I wouldn't get past the first few years because I did it."

But Fran did get past the first few years. In fact, he proved himself to be perhaps the most durable quarterback of all time. In fact, he did not miss a game because of injury until the 1977 season!

"There's no explanation for it that I can see," said Fran, who, as the NFL record-holder for most yards rushing (3,674) for a quarterback, absorbed a good deal

"The Scrambler" does his thing.

of punishment. "The only thing I can see is that different players are, for one reason or another, able to play when they're hurt. Jim Marshall [his Viking teammate] has probably the most phenomenal record I've ever heard of in professional football—a defensive end starting more than 200 straight games. I've seen him with unbelievable injuries, but he's played and he continues to play."

Fran added, "Bad injuries, the incapacitating ones like Namath has had, you just can't play with. . . . I've gotten hit, but I've just been lucky. You survive it somehow. The only meaningful explanation is, if you don't get completely incapacitated, you play with some hurts."

Having shouldered so much criticism throughout his career (even his first coach, Norm Van Brocklin, criticized his style), Fran is justifiably proud of his unparalleled accomplishments as a quarterback.

"I find it very interesting as I get to this point in my career," remarked Fran once in his twilight years, as his name was becoming more and more prominent in the record books. "I find it very rewarding because I think you have to look at the data of what people do and not what you think they can do or what you think their limitations are from the standpoint of size and strength. And I think the data is coming through quite well."

That's an understatement if there ever was one. "The data" hasn't come through better for any quarterback in NFL history. The name Tarkenton virtually monopolizes the NFL passing records. His achievements include: most passing attempts, career, 6,467; most passing completions, career, 3,686; most passes attempted, season, 572; most passes completed, season 345; most yards passing, career, 47,003; most touchdown passes, career, 342; and most seasons passing for 2,000 or more yards, 16.

There's no question that Fran's astounding success

revolutionized the role of quarterback. Gradually, the old conception of the classic pocket passer has fallen by the wayside. "The idea of a scrambler," Fran said, "is *now* perfectly acceptable. A lot of quarterbacks do it—Griese, Bradshaw, Jones—but in 1961, when I came into the league, I must have looked like some kind of lunatic loping around back there, especially in contrast to the established quarterbacks, most of whom were about as mobile as 16-inch shore batteries."

Tarkenton had little choice but to scramble when he first joined the Vikings. An expansion club, the Vikes simply didn't have the power up front to give Fran time to throw. So instead of playing sitting duck, he played waterbug—skittering, scrambling, and running.

He had immediate success, even if people were too busy criticizing him to notice. Although Fran started his rookie year on the bench, he replaced veteran George Shaw midway through the first game. "Fran the Scram" went on to throw four touchdown passes to spark the upstart Vikings to a 37–13 triumph over the Chicago Bears. He finished the year with 18 touchdown tosses, only two shy of Charley Conerly's mark for a rookie. The Vikes, meanwhile, wound up at 3–11—not all that bad for an expansion club.

In 1962, after another year of growing pains (though Fran pitched 22 scoring passes), the Vikings improved to 5–8–1 in their third year of existence. The former University of Georgia All-American led the way, completing over 57 percent of his passes for 2,311 yards and 15 touchdowns.

The Vikes were the talk of football in 1964. The young club jumped to 8–5–1, good for a second-place tie with the powerful Green Bay Packers. Tarkenton excelled again. He threw for 2,506 yards and 22 touchdowns, while connecting on 56 percent of his passes. Not bad for a scrambler.

But the Vikings' startling success did not continue. A disappointing 7–7 finish in 1965 was followed by an even-more-disappointing 4–9–1 mark in 1966. Fran had good years, but the team did not win. By 1967, Fran had begun the second phase of his career. He became quarterback of the hapless New York Giants. Assuming the reins of a team that had finished 1–12–1 the year before, Fran was essentially working with an expansion club all over again.

His impact was immediate—and remarkable. In one year, Tarkenton transformed an inept offense into an explosive, high-powered unit that was third best in the league. He gunned for a career-high 29 touchdown passes and 3,088 yards passing. He also rushed for 306 yards—an average of 7 yards per carry. The Giants vaulted to 7–7 and a second-place finish in their division.

Following a few more seasons of about .500 ball, Tarkenton led the Giants to a 9–5 mark in 1970. The team just missed qualifying for the playoffs. Francis finally seemed to be getting some long-deserved praise. "A lot of quarterbacks look more impressive and throw the ball harder," noted writer Joseph Agresta, "but few, if any, do more for their team than Francis Tarkenton."

But the kind words did not last for long. Mostly due to the NFL's weak defense, the Giants slumped to 4–10 in 1970. Feeling that a change of scenery would do him good, Tarkenton asked to be traded.

In 1972, Fran pulled on a familiar purple jersey. He was back in Minnesota. Sorely in need of an offensive leader, the Vikings gave up three players and two draft choices to reacquire Number 10. It was one of the best deals they ever made.

After one .500 season, Tarkenton led the Vikings to six consecutive divisional titles and three NFC titles. Over that span, they amassed a regular-season record of 62–22–2. Hardly the mark of a .500 quarterback.

Still, Tarkenton's critics persisted. They pointed out that he had failed to win a Super Bowl in three tries.

"I don't think any individual wins the Super Bowl, and I don't think any individual loses the Super Bowl," responded Francis. "That's a team goal.... A lot of things happen. It's not an easy thing. You can have the best team and not win it. You can have a lesser team and win it.

"Those things happen all the time," continued Fran. "There is tremendous disappointment, but then you realize it's the nature of our sport. It happens to a lot of teams and a lot of players. It happens every year."

A thoughtful, intelligent man, Tarkenton always seemed to be able to keep the criticism he received in perspective. "Every quarterback worth his salt has been criticized during his career," Fran noted. "It's the nature of the position; it's a love-hate position. Everybody has an opinion on the quarterback.

"I was on an expansion team those first six years. How many expansion teams have come up and won championships? When I left those expansion teams, I went to a team that was 1–12–1 and worse than an expansion team.

"I thought I helped lend some respectability to the Giants because, all of a sudden, we were 7–7, 7–7, 6–8, and 9–5, which is the best period they've had since their championship years. I felt a great personal sense of accomplishment. But no one else did, because they said, 'He's still a .500 quarterback.'

"But I understood all that," Fran went on. "I knew and felt all along that on the proper team I'd be able to make the proper contribution to winning championships."

Fran received an undue amount of criticism from the press and fans. But what did the players and coaches— the men whose opinions *really* count—think of him?

"He's impossible to defense," declared Jim Carter, Green Bay's middle linebacker. "Whatever you have geared up to stop them, Tarkenton just finds something else. He sees everything on the field the second the ball is snapped."

Fred Dryer, the Los Angeles Rams' defensive end and a former teammate of Fran's, said, "I've played with Fran and I've played against him, and he does things for a team you wouldn't believe. He sprints out, he throws to his backs, he varies his play selection and he has an excellent feel for the game itself. He can sense what's going to work and what's not going to work.... He's just moving and sliding on you all the time. He can feel if there's a man behind him. He's a very cunning-type quarterback with a lot of instincts going for him.... He'll win any way he can. For one thing, he and Billy Kilmer can play catchup football better than anybody. He can pick you apart with short passes if he has to, or devastate you with the bomb."

Green Bay Coach and Hall-of-Fame quarterback Bart Starr added, "For years, Francis was getting rapped for his scrambling and unorthodox tactics. Good qualities were overlooked. He is an amazingly accurate passer, an extremely sharp tactician, always in complete control."

Bud Grant, the Vikings coach, has called Tarkenton "the greatest quarterback ever." Several years ago, the coach accurately predicted, "He's going to win all the statistics when he's through. But his greatest single asset is his enthusiasm for every part of the game. He is

Francis stayed in the pocket, too. Here he unleashes an 80-yard touchdown bomb to John Gilliam.

interested in every other player and every other team. He is not a doubter, but a doer. When he calls a play, he has a vision of what every player, his and the other team's, will do."

Fran's retirement caught some people by surprise, especially because he had such a brilliant year in 1978. He became the first passer in NFL history to complete more than 300 passes in a season (he had 345), in addition to throwing for a career-high 3,468 yards.

"I could have played another year," disclosed Tarkenton, "but I did not want to go out of the game as a lame-duck quarterback. Last year, I had what I consider my most productive year. I contributed more to my team than any year that I played."

Francis is philosophical about his record-breaking, 18-year career. "I've had fun. I've had heartache. I've been beaten. I've won."

Of the criticism he labored under for so long, he said, "I don't look back with any malice or vindictiveness. It's like many American stories. You like to read those stories and you like to be a part of them. I wasn't even drafted in the first round. Unitas wasn't either. From the day you come up and you're too small and not strong enough, and then you can accomplish some things, it's meaningful. It's like you defied the so-called experts, whoever they may be."

Nobody ever defied them better than Francis Asbury Tarkenton. And you can look it up—in the NFL record books—if you don't believe it.

O. J. SIMPSON

"O. J. is more than a football player. He's the hottest item in sports. His charisma cuts across generations." These are the words of former general manager of the San Francisco 49'ers, Joe Thomas. Indeed, in the course of his pro-football career, Simpson has become America's most visible sports personality. Intelligent, personable, and good-looking, O. J. began popping up everywhere—and not only on the football field.

He appeared in such movies as *The Towering Inferno, Capricorn One,* and *Firepower.* Through his promotional assignments for a car-rental company, he became known as the "Superstar in Rent-a-Car." And he has also made numerous appearances on network television shows.

But Orenthal James Simpson was a superstar on the football field long before he was the "Superstar in Rent-a-Car." Hailed as a once-in-a-generation running back after two sensational All-American years at the University of Southern California, O. J. was the first player selected in the 1969 draft. His record was perfect. In his two years at USC (he had previously attended junior college in San Francisco, where he scored 54 touchdowns and rushed for 2,445 yards), O. J. amassed the staggering total of 3,124 yards and 35 touchdowns.

He was supposed to be the savior of the lowly Buffalo Bills, who were coming off a 1–12–1 season. But things didn't go according to plan.

After holding out for a good part of his rookie preseason because of a contract dispute, O. J. joined a deeply troubled team. Once a powerhouse in the American Football League, the Bills of 1969 were a team divided. In one corner were the aging veterans, the holdovers from the glory years. In the other corner were the younger players. The two factions did not mix comfortably.

But for O. J., the biggest problem was that Coach John Rauch didn't believe a pro running back could be effective running the ball 30 or 40 times a game, as O. J. had in college. NFL defenses could key on the player too easily that way, Rauch felt. He wanted to use Simpson more as a receiver and blocker.

Always a forthright man, O. J. disagreed with his coach. "Let me run, and I'll make Buffalo a winner," proclaimed O. J. But O. J. didn't run much, and the Bills didn't win much. It was not a great start for the most heralded rookie running back in NFL history. Averaging only 13 carries per game, Simpson picked up 697 yards.

O. J.'s sophomore season started off much better. He maintained nearly a 1,000-yard pace through the first seven games. But then he sustained a knee injury, which sidelined him for the rest of the year.

The Bills hit a new low in 1971 under a new coach, Harvey Johnson. They finished with the worst record in the NFL, 1–13. It was small consolation to O. J. that he had his best season, gaining 742 yards. He was not a happy football player. Simpson still felt misused or, more accurately, underused.

Three disappointing seasons into what was supposed

A healthy O. J. airborne against the Browns.

to be a glittering career, O. J. had yet to fulfill his enormous potential. But his confidence remained unshaken. He still believed that all he needed was the chance to carry the ball more often.

Presto! Enter Lou Saban, the former Bills' coach, who returned in 1972. "We know you're a great running back," Saban told O. J., "and we're going to give you the ball as often as we can." And to give O. J. some holes to run through, Saban made it his top priority to get strong blockers.

Winning four games, the rebuilding Bills weren't exactly the talk of the league in 1972. But O. J. Simpson was! At long last the focal point of the Buffalo offense, O. J. responded by leading the league in rushing with 1,251 yards. After breaking the 100-yard mark in only three games in his first three years, Simpson did it six times in 1972.

The real O. J. Simpson had stood up. The rest, as they say, is history.

All O. J. did the following year, 1973, was to have the greatest season a running back has ever had. He got off to a blazing start, romping for a record 250 yards in the season opener against the New England Patriots. He followed that performance with four straight 100-yards-plus games. Through five games, he had already rushed for 813 yards. He was ahead of the pace Jimmy Brown had maintained in 1963, the year he set the all-time NFL season rushing mark of 1,863 yards.

For a long time, that record had been considered untouchable. But it had been a long time since any runner had had the kind of year O. J. was having. NFL fans from coast to coast began watching Simpson's performances. "Can O. J. surpass the great Jimmy Brown?" people wondered.

Pressure mounted by the week. After picking up only 55 yards against the world-champion Miami Dolphins, Simpson came back to race for 157 against the Kansas City Chiefs in game seven. In only half a year, O. J. had passed the 1,000-yard mark, a milestone that usually takes even the finest backs a whole season to achieve. And here he was cruising on a 2,000-yard course. It was an unheard of record—but something O. J. had dreamed about since his rookie year. The race for the record resumed. O. J. was relentless in his pursuit. He was held to 79 and 99 yards in his next two games, but then he burst for four straight over-100-yards days. After 12 games, his total was 1,584. Only two games remained. O. J. still needed 280 yards to pass Brown. His chances seemed slim. And 2,000 was now out of the question.

Or was it? Playing in a near-blizzard in Buffalo's Rich Stadium, O. J. ran wild in the next-to-last game of the year. On only 21 carries, the "Juice" riddled the Patriots for 219 yards! Brown's "untouchable" record was now only 63 yards away.

"We'll get it," vowed offensive guard Reggie McKenzie, an outstanding lineman and close friend of O. J.'s. "We'll get it if we have to run Juice 64 times."

The stage was set. "The Electric Company," as McKenzie dubbed the Bills' line (because "We turn the Juice loose"), was determined to help their teammate get the record. The dramatic chase came to New York, where the Bills would play the Jets.

It was snowing in New York. "When I saw the snow, I felt bad," related O. J. later. "But then I remembered it snowed the week before in Buffalo, and everything turned out okay."

Everything wasn't okay this time...everything was fabulous! O. J. ended the season-long drama in the first

115

quarter. Spurting through a big hole, he darted for six yards—and a total of 1,864 yards. O. J. had done it! But the celebration was restrained. There was another "impossible" milestone to shoot for.

Down after down, O. J. dashed through the Jet defense. By the time the fourth quarter began, he was only 60 yards shy of the magic number—2,000.

In constant communication with statisticians in the press box, the Bills' quarterback Joe Ferguson knew exactly how much O. J. needed. "The Juice only needs 60," said Ferguson to his teammates as the final quarter of the season began. Everybody knew what he meant.

O. J. chopped off 21 of those yards on a drive early in the fourth quarter. But the Jet defense stiffened, and the Bills were forced to punt. The New York fans booed. They were as eager as everybody else to see history made.

The Bills got the ball back. O. J. scooted around right end for 22 yards. After being stopped up the middle, he went left for a 9-yard gain. In the huddle, Ferguson was not only calling plays, he was also doing arithmetic, keeping precise tabs on how much O. J. needed.

The quarterback sent fullback Jim Braxton up the middle on two straight plays. The fans booed some more, but O. J. needed a quick breather. Juice got the next call, and whipped around the left again, this time for five. Only four yards to go.

Ferguson relayed the latest figures, and called for play Number 5, which had O. J. carrying up the middle behind Braxton, one of the finest blocking backs in the game. The hole was there. O. J. hit it in a flash. He slashed for seven yards. That did it!

"Was that hole big enough for you?" asked Braxton, sporting an ear-to-ear grin. Practically before he could get up, O. J. was mobbed by the entire Buffalo team, which carried him off the field as the appreciative New York fans responded with a deafening ovation. On the sidelines, O. J. embraced Lou Saban, the coach who had rescued his career.

Afterward, in a conference room packed with some 400 reporters and photographers, O. J. brought the Bills' entire offensive unit with him to share the moment of glory.

"I want to introduce the cats who've done the job for me all year," said the new rushing champion, humbly. "It's their record as much as mine." O. J. introduced his teammates individually, taking a special moment longer for McKenzie, whom he always refers to as "my main man." It was McKenzie who, much earlier in the season, had whispered to O. J., "Why don't we go for 2,000?"

"He's one heckuva man," McKenzie said emotionally a little later. "I mean, who else do you know would take the entire line to a national press conference the way he did? He's just beautiful.

"The man is the greatest in the world at what he does," McKenzie continued. "That's Number 1. All athletes respect greatness. But Number 2, the man does not dish out any jive. He doesn't brush off people who aren't stars, who don't start."

Along with the *big* one, O. J. set a number of other NFL records in that memorable 1973 season, including: most yards gained, game, 250 (a record he later broke with 273 yards in 1976); most consecutive games, 100 or more yards rushing, season, 7; most games, 100 or more yards rushing, season, 11; most games, 200 or more yards rushing, season, 3; and most consecutive games, 200 or more yards rushing, 2.

Having established himself as the finest runner in the game—indeed, of all time—with his record-shattering

1973 season, O. J. was merely mortal in 1974. He ran for "only" 1,125 yards that year. But he was back in record-breaking territory in 1975, gaining 1,817 yards. After picking up another 1,503 in 1976, O. J. was less than 3,000 yards away from Brown's all-time career rushing record of 12,312.

But then injuries struck. Limited to a half-season by a knee injury, O. J. had just 557 yards in 1977. It was after that season that Simpson was traded to the 49'ers. It was a swap O. J. pushed for, and he can thank Bills' owner Ralph Wilson for accommodating his wishes. As badly as he wanted to keep Simpson, Wilson let him go, purely out of respect for O. J. "He wanted to play on the West Coast," said Wilson in announcing the deal, "where he had many personal ties. And at this stage of his career, he deserves that opportunity."

Often superstars and their owners are adversaries. But it wasn't that way with Simpson and Wilson. They respected each other a great deal. "He's as great a person as he is a football player," Wilson once said of O. J.

In 1978, the Juice's uniform may have changed, but the injuries remained. Simpson returned to the Bay City, his home town. But the homecoming was hardly triumphant. For both O. J. and the 49'ers, 1978 was a disappointment.

Plagued with chronic knee problems and a shoulder injury, O. J. saw limited action and gained 593 yards, a more-than-respectable total for most running backs. But O. J. is not most running backs.

Meanwhile, injuries to a number of other key players spelled doom for the talented but inexperienced 49'ers, the second youngest team in the NFL. The result was a

The Juice high-steps against the Giants.

2–14 finish, the worst season in the 28-year history of the team.

But in 1979, the new coach of the 49'ers, Bill Walsh, said, "We know what O. J. can do. He is one of the great runners in the history of the game, and we hope to have him back and healthy in 1979." And as for O. J., there is still one record he would like to beat: his career rushing total of 10,776 leaves him 1,536 short of Brown's record. It's a mark O. J. would love to have. But one thing is certain: O. J. is not going to hang on just for the sake of records. He wants to be remembered for his blinding speed, his lightning-fast moves, and his breathtaking runs, not for one record.

"The thing is," says O. J., "I want to leave the game like Jim Brown—who quit while he was still the best."

Whether O. J. can overtake Brown remains to be seen. But whatever happens, there's no question that they are the two greatest running backs in NFL history. Perhaps someday Walter Payton or Tony Dorsett will join their select company. But for now, Simpson and Brown are the yardsticks by which other runners are measured. It couldn't be any other way. Between them, Simpson, the graceful sprinter and slasher, and Brown, the awesome and agile powerhouse, hold every rushing record imaginable.

O. J. likes to tell a story about him and Jimmy Brown. The year was 1962. The place was Kezar Stadium in San Francisco. Brown had just rushed for 135 yards and 2 touchdowns against the 49'ers. He ran into a cocky 15-year-old kid at a nearby ice cream parlor after the game. The kid was O. J. Simpson.

"The other kids were really awed when he walked in,"

O. J. recalled with a smile. "But you know, I was the leader of the gang, so I had to say something."

"Jim Brown, you ain't so great," said the brash youngster, making sure his friends could hear. "When I get to play pro ball, I'm going to break all your records."

Brown smiled and responded quietly, "You talk big now, but let's see what you do when you get the chance."

O. J. laughs when he tells the story. "Now kids are always coming up to me just like that and saying they're going to break all *my* records. So I tell them what Jim Brown told me."

"The fact is," continues the Juice, "someday, somebody will."

Someday, maybe, but not for awhile.